WORKING LIVES

Shops

Cherry Gilchrist

B. T. BATSFORD LTD   LONDON

© Cherry Gilchrist 1986
First published 1986

All right reserved. No part of this publication may be reproduced, in any form or by any means, without permission from the Publisher

Typeset by Tek-Art Ltd, Kent
and printed in Great Britain by
R.J. Acford
Chichester, Sussex
for the publishers
B.T. Batsford Ltd,
4 Fitzhardinge Street,
London W1H 0AH

ISBN 0 7134 5151 3

Cover illustrations
The black and white print shows an early nineteenth-century draper's shop (Guildhall Library); the portrait is of a shopkeeper in the 1950s (Beamish North of England Open Air Museum); the colour photograph shows a check-out in a modern supermarket (John Lewis Partnership Archive Collection).

Frontispiece
A typical sweet-shop of the 1950s.

Acknowledgments
The Author and Publishers would like to thank the following for their kind permission to reproduce copyright illustrations: Beamish North of England Open Air Museum for the frontispiece and figures 4, 16, 18, 19, 23, 24, 27, 38 and 41; Elstons', Minehead for figure 46; Guildhall Library for figures 3, 5, 11, 14, 29 and 36; Heal's for figures 28, 30, 34 and 44; House of Fraser for figures 10, 12, 13, 15, 20, 31, 32, 33, 39, 40, 43 and 45; John Lewis Partnership Archive Collection for figures 6, 9, 17, 35, 42 and 49; Marks & Spencer for figures 7, 8, 26 and 50; People's Palace, Glasgow Museums for figure 2; A.D. Peters & Co. Ltd for figure 48; Ridler's Shoe Shop, Minehead for figure 25; Woolworth's, Minehead for figure 22. Figures 1, 21, 37 and 47 are from the Author's collection.

The Author would like to give her special thanks to all those who have contributed their memories to this book.

Contents

List of Illustrations 4
Introduction 5

1 Shops Before the First World War 8
2 War and Peace: 1914-30 18
3 The 1930s: Science in Selling 26
4 Wartime and the Post-War Period 34
5 The 1950s and 1960s: Shopping for Convenience 46
6 The 1970s and On: the Electronic Age 54

Glossary 61
Date List 62
Books for Further Reading 63
Index 64

List of Illustrations

1	Market sign	5
2	Eighteenth-century shop	6
3	Upper-class shop, 1809	7
4	Selling from a horse-drawn cart	8
5	A perfume shop	9
6	An apprenticeship indenture	10
7	Michael Marks and Thomas Spencer	11
8	'Penny Bazaar' stall	12
9	Bond's annual staff outing, 1901	13
10	Howell's shop assistants, 1910	14
11	The demand for a half day's holiday	15
12	A bill of 1888	16
13	A ladies' rest room, 1924	20
14	'The Spirit of the House'	21
15	Howell's staff outing, 1925	22
16	A tailor's shop	22
17	John Lewis's grocery department, 1922	23
18	A haberdasher's shop, 1930	24
19	A hat shop	24
20	A 'genteel' tea room, 1924	25
21	*Punch* cartoon, 1932	26
22	Woolworth's staff keep fit display	27
23	A window display in Hexham	28
24	The arrival of radio	29
25	A shoe shop display	29
26	A new Marks and Spencer's store of the 1930s	30
27	A delivery boy from a butcher's shop	31
28	Heal's horse-drawn delivery van	32
29	Selfridge's Staff Guide Book	33
30	Heal's Home Guard	34
31	Shopping for Valentine cards	35
32	Helping the war effort	36
33	A.R.P. wardens at Brown and Muff's	37
34	The parachute factory at Heal's	38
35	'Business as usual'	39
36	Gamage's store after an air-raid	40
37	Post-war shortages	42
38	A chemist at work in his shop	44
39	Hammond's new store, 1950s	46
40	A window-dresser at work	47
41	An electrical shop	48
42	Waitrose new self-service supermarket	49
43	The hat and coat department at Cavendish's	50
44	The staff magazine at Heal's	52
45	A children's party, 1958	53
46	The laser scanning check-out system	55
47	A part-time music shop	56
48	Posy Simmons' cartoon	56
49	Working at a food counter	58
50	Marks and Spencer's hairdressing service	60

Introduction

Britain has been called 'a nation of shopkeepers', and it is true that there have always been many people keen to start their own retail business and a public that enjoys shopping as a social activity as well as out of necessity. There have been shops in this country since mediaeval times, but for many centuries much of the trading was done through markets, which were held regularly in the town centre or on a grand scale once a year. Certain products, such as shoes, clothes and furniture, were usually bought direct from the craftsmen and women who made them, and other, smaller items, such as ribbons and gloves, were taken from house to house by travelling pedlars.

In the last 300 years, though, it has become

1 *In the old tradition of selling goods at market, the vendors had to pay a 'toll' to the local council, as this nineteenth-century sign from Lyme Regis, Dorset, shows.*

2 Painting of a small eighteenth-century Glasgow shop, artist unknown. The cone-shaped packages are loaves of sugar, and it looks as though the female shopkeeper sold only the most basic provisions.

more common to buy goods from fixed shops. These can be defined as buildings or rooms where a permanent display of items is on show, and into which the customer can walk and be served by the owner or his assistant. During the nineteenth century these ranged from the humble front parlour in which home-made sweets were sold, to palatial 'emporiums' catering for the 'carriage trade', the rich customers who arrived by horse and carriage. These were often designed to look as much like stately homes as possible, thereby making these wealthy customers feel at home and taking away the rather disagreeable atmosphere of 'trade'. The aristocracy felt that shopkeeping was a low-class occupation, however expensive the goods on sale. The assistants were required to wait upon them like the best-trained servants.

This book will look at the work of people in shops from late Victorian times until the present

3 A shop for the upper classes, as depicted in 1809. Notice how it resembles a stately home in its layout. An assistant can be seen ushering in a lady customer.

day. During this time, the work of the small village shopkeeper has probably changed the least, whereas in the towns various innovations have caused major changes for workers in the retail trade. These include the rise of the department store, which set shopping on a larger scale than ever before, the coming of 'multiple' or 'chain' stores (such as Woolworth's, and Marks and Spencer's) and the arrival of the supermarket. All these, as we shall see, have come about as part of the general pattern of social change. Shopping habits are affected by the transport available, the amount of money customers have to spend, and the kind of products that the manufacturers can offer.

The term 'shop-worker' covers a wide variety of jobs, from that of shopkeeper, to counter hand, to stock controller, to general manager, to name but a few. In this book, the emphasis is largely upon the work of the general sales assistant, but it also takes into account shop management, and the position of the shopkeeper running his or her own business. During the last hundred years the status of the shop assistant has declined; once viewed as a respectable and desirable career for a working-class or lower middle-class person, it does not now carry such prestige. However, working conditions have improved out of all recognition. At the turn of the century, assistants had very little personal freedom and worked extremely long hours for low pay. Today, welfare facilities are good, and employees have many more rights, such as equal pay for men and women, the right to appeal against unfair dismissal, and a minimum scale of wages. We will be looking at how the pattern of work in shops has evolved in relation to the social and economic climate and to developing technology.

1 Shops Before the First World War

By the beginning of this century, shops in Britain ranged from tiny 'parlour' shops in private houses to huge, luxurious department stores serving thousands of customers a day. And the people working in these shops varied greatly in their age, background and skills. There were young apprentices, skilled craftsmen and women, smartly-turned out sales assistants, hawk-eyed managers and seasonal workers. A shop-owner could be anybody from a rather slow, elderly lady selling a few groceries to the proprietor of a grand store who considered himself lord of his empire and of all who worked there.

Among this wide variety of shops and shopworkers certain patterns of work which characterize the late Victorian and the Edwardian period can be picked out. To begin with, there was still a strong tradition that retailing involved not only selling goods but producing them as well. Although the Industrial Revolution had started the process of mass production, so that all kinds of hardware, materials, and fancy goods could be turned out cheaply by machines in factories for subsequent sale in shops, still the old methods of making items and selling them direct persisted. Boots and shoes, dresses, perfumes, jewellery, sweets, puddings and pies could still be bought on the premises where they had been made.

The craftsman as retailer

Craft and retailing existed side by side in both large and small businesses. In 1914, for instance, in Shropshire, an old man carried on a trade of making sweets and then selling them to local villagers or by trundling them off on a hand-cart to market. His 'factory' stood behind the country cottage in which he lived.

4 Many tradesmen, like this butcher, travelled about to sell their provisions from a horse-drawn cart.

THE ROYAL LABORATORY OF FLOWERS.

FLOWER FARMS AND STILLS AT MITCHAM, SURREY.

FLOWER FARMS AND STILLS AT NICE, AND GRASSE.

VIENNA 1873. 2, NEW BOND STREET, LONDON. PARIS, 1871.
Export Bonded Factory, "B" Warehouse, St. Katharine Dock.
VIENNA. 1873.

Inside it was warm with the glow of the fire and fragrant with the aroma of peppermint, almonds, chocolate and all sorts of mouthwatering smells. A huge brick stove with a blackened iron top stood at one end and on it several large pans bubbled away merrily. (*The Countryman Book of Village Trades and Crafts,* 1978)

Dairymen who sold milk were often cow-keepers as well. Although in the larger towns dairy-owners usually bought the milk they were to sell from farmers, and, increasingly, had it sent to them by rail, in smaller towns and villages, and even still in some city shops, cows were kept and milked in stalls at the back of the premises! There was little or no attempt at hygiene, and customers would bring their own jugs to be filled. It was common practice, too, for the sharp trader to water down the milk. In 1901 legislation was brought in to try and stop these tricks, but it was not until the 1930s that laws were passed to ensure that milk was clean and free from infection.

5 *A perfume shop of the late nineteenth century. The assistants are dressed as smartly as their customers, but do not wear hats.*

Today's shoe shops which offer a repair service are a survival of the shops where boots and shoes were made by hand. Here, the craftsmen would usually be separated from the assistants who served the public, and the making of the shoes would be carried out in a workshop set apart from the sales area. Shopkeepers were proud of offering this service, since factory-made shoes were usually of poor quality and were bought chiefly by the working classes:

Mr A C Quick, Boot and Shoe Mfr. 2 Church Square. A large bespoke trade is done, ladies' and gentlemen's boots, etc., being turned out to order in good style, fit and finish. All descriptions of repairs are promptly executed by experienced craftsmen. (*Guernsey Illustrated,* 1896)

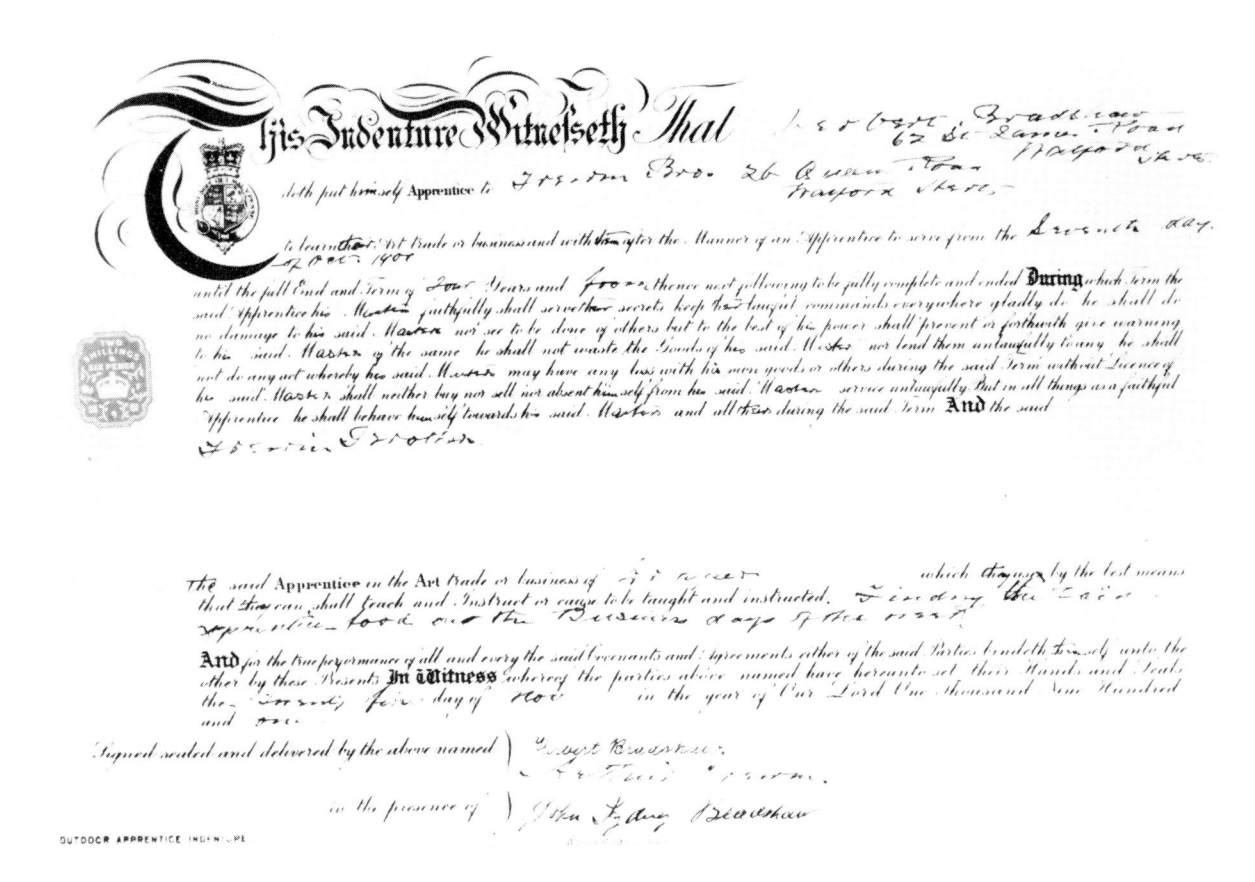

6 *An apprenticeship indenture, which was the legal document binding a new recruit to his or her employers, in this case for a term of four years*

Dressmakers' shops

Before the First World War, few items of clothing were made in factories. Dressmakers and tailors had their own shops, and in the larger stores there were workrooms where dozens of girls might be employed in cutting-out, stitching and finishing-off customers' orders. Parents of working-class and lower middle-class girls often considered this an excellent career for their daughters, since they would be highly trained and their working conditions cleaner and more socially acceptable than those of a factory. These girls were usually apprenticed, so that they undertook to work for the firm for several years and be paid little or nothing in order to learn the art and skills of sewing. The following is a letter from the manager of Brown and Muff's store, Bradford, to Mrs Rhodes, dated January 1913:

Dear Madam,
  With reference to your application, re your daughter, we agree to engage her for three years' apprenticeship in the millinery workroom, terms as stated, to begin with 2/6d per week, and should be glad if she would come on Feb 17th. Trusting the benefit will be mutual.

  Margaret Penn, with two years' dressmaking experience, was offered an apprenticeship at a fashionable Manchester store in about 1912, when she was a teenager. However, her family could not afford for her to take this up, as she would have been paid nothing for the first three years. She was taken on as an 'errand girl' instead, which gave her a wage of 5s. a week and the chance to be taught many of the skills of dressmaking as well. In her autobiography, *Manchester Fourteen Miles* (1947), in which she calls herself 'Hilda', she writes:

The one and only thing she actively disliked

about her daily routine was picking up the countless pins which the young ladies in the workroom dropped so continually and carelessly .... Even so she counted it a small price to pay for the glory of becoming a Court dressmaker in the highest-class shop in Manchester.

She was initiated into the process of making garments in several stages; first she sewed inside seams, then was allowed to make buttonholes and, finally, as a great privilege, was given a pocket to cut out under strict supervision:

Hilda worked carefully, the big cutting-out scissors feeling like shears in her trembling hands. Miss Robinson, watching kindly, said it was all right and she had taken the first step up the ladder.

Department, major and multiple stores

Department stores were a major feature of shopping by this time. The idea had originated in France in the 1860s and, during the late nineteenth and early twentieth century, major stores, such as Selfridge's (London), Bentall's (Kingston-upon-Thames) and Brown and Chester's (Chester), were set up in Britain. Many department stores had started off as small family businesses, usually drapers, and had expanded when the owners bought up other property or had palatial new premises built. At Barker's of Kensington, for instance, John Barker had, by 1893, bought up 28 other shops and established 42 departments. He employed more than 1000 staff and kept 80 horses in the stables to cope with deliveries. Department stores were introduced mainly to provide leisurely and luxurious shopping for the middle and upper classes. Like the earlier, smaller shops which had served the aristocracy, they were designed to look like stately homes, and the shop assistants were expected to wait on the customers with as much deference as their personal butlers and maids would have done.

Other large shops, which specialized in one particular type of goods, such as Heal's (furniture) and Liberty's (oriental materials and ornaments),

---

7 *Michael Marks and Thomas Spencer, who founded their famous partnership by opening market stalls in northern England in the late nineteenth century*

8 *One of their 'Penny Bazaar' stalls in Cardiff market, 1901. By this time they owned about 12 shops and 24 covered market stalls throughout the country.*

were also coming into prominence. And 'multiple' or 'chain' stores were mushrooming. Marks and Spencer's, starting as a 'Penny Bazaar' in Wigan market hall in 1891, had expanded to 60 branches by 1907. In department, major and multiple stores, assistants worked in a strict hierarchy, their dress, duties, and conduct governed closely by shop policy and rules.

A 'respectable' job

Even though life as a shop assistant could be very hard, it was considered better than industrial or agricultural work and working in a shop was said to be respectable. Some of the lower classes did sneer at their contemporaries who had jobs in shops, calling them 'counter-jumpers' if they tried to ingratiate themselves with their well-to-do customers, even though these same customers treated the assistants with haughty disdain much of the time.

Getting work

Getting temporary work in a shop was easy at certain times of the year, since employers took on extra assistants for the busy periods and then sacked them as soon as trade slackened. Some proprietors, such as the notorious William Whiteley, of Whiteley's, London, exploited the

9 *The annual staff outing was a treat much looked forward to by shop assistants, in this case from Bond's of Norwich, 1911.*

hopes of unemployed Welsh and Irish workers by advertising in their local papers for staff. Queues would form outside the store, whereupon Mr Whiteley himself would appear:

His formula when engaging was the same for all. 'Good morning, young man . . . . I have vacancies in my linen, furnishing, oriental, dress and country order departments – supposing I was to engage you . . . . We ask for no references, we give no references. There is one moment's notice on either side . . . . What is the lowest possible salary you will take?' (P.C. Hoffman, *They Also Serve*, 1949)

The 'boss'

Despite the enormous size of these retailing concerns, the boss, or a junior member of his family, was prominent in shop affairs and kept an eye on matters. Many were better liked than William Whiteley. Mrs A. Rozzell recalls her working days at John Lewis:

A tall handsome young man who often strode along the gangway to a desk at the extreme end of the room (often calling out in a deep voice as he passed 'Less noise please') immediately excited my curiosity. In answer to my enquiry I was told he was Mr Spedan Lewis and very much liked in spite of the fact that most people stood in considerable awe of him. (*John Lewis Gazette*, 1959)

A number of these employers, having built up their business totally by their own efforts and anxious themselves to cross the great gap between the middle and upper classes, bought their way into the aristocracy as best they could. ('Trade' was still frowned upon as an occupation by the upper classes.) Arthur Liberty, founder of Liberty's in Regent Street, London, had a marble seat built for himself at Marylebone Station, to sit on while waiting for the train to take him home to his new country mansion, Lee Manor. At home he took on the role of the Lord of the Manor, and each year the staff of his shop were invited to spend a day there.

10 *A group of shop assistants, dressed in regulation black, at Howell's, Cardiff, around 1910*

Dress and conduct

Dress for shop staff at this period was normally black, and assistants, in particular, were expected to be smart and neat in appearance. Male assistants sometimes wore morning coats, striped trousers, and stiff collars. In grocers' shops, black or white cotton uniforms were often worn. Assistants were also required to be quiet, discreet and decorous in their manner – but this was not always easy:

At the Home and Colonial Stores . . . the tea was weighed and packed by boys and young men dressed in chefs' hats, standing in the window so all might see how everything was fair, square and above board. It provided also a perennial source of delight, as well as an excellent test of their sex-appeal, for girls to look closely in at the window and enjoy the blushes of the boys and mayhap blush back as some less susceptible lad winked wickedly. (*They Also Serve*)

Working hours

Conditions in shops varied greatly, but in general the hours worked were very long. The average is estimated to have been between 75 and 90 hours a week, which included helping to clean up, dust, put out and put away stock. Once gas lighting had become available by the late nineteenth century, there was no need for shops to close when it got dark, and shopkeepers started to compete with each other by staying open later and later. Margaret Bondfield, who was later to campaign for better conditions for shop assistants, remembered that when she was employed as an assistant, she would be sent out at night:

. . . to scout around and see if the shops over the way showed any signs of closing; if they did we, too, would hastily and gladly put up the shutters.
(Quoted in *Victorian Ladies at Work* by Lee Holcombe)

11 *The cover of a popular song, designed to arouse support for the shop assistants' demand for a half day's holiday each week*

As early as 1842, a campaign was started by the Early Closing Association to introduce a half holiday a week (most assistants worked a six-day week) and to shorten shop opening hours. Despite bills presented in Parliament, and growing evidence of how shop-workers were exploited, nothing effective was done about this until the First World War. In 1886 young people under the age of 18 received some protection, but this seems ludicrous by today's standards: they were restricted to working 'only' 74 hours a week.

Pay

By the late nineteenth century, pay ranged from about 7s. a week for a woman working in a lower-class shop, to £1 a week for one in a fashionable London store. Some stores operated a commission system, whereby assistants were expected to make up their wage by the small percentage they received of the price of goods they themselves were responsible for selling to customers. Even in this, however, there was a pecking order: when a customer entered a shop, the most senior assistant would serve him or her, and only when all the other assistants were fully occupied could the newest and most junior assistant take a turn at serving. Holiday pay was unknown; at John Lewis's, for instance, the first holiday pay that assistants remember being given was for Queen Victoria's funeral!

In many shops, fines were imposed, which could reduce the meagre pay to almost nothing. The *Daily Chronicle* published its investigation into the conditions of shop-workers in 1898 and, among other hardships, found that one assistant had been fined 5s. for leaving meat on his plate at a mealtime, and another 2s. 6d. for coming back late after lunch. Rules from Hammond's in Hull (*c* 1880) include the following:

11. **For each article left out of parcel.**
    For omitting own number on bill.
    For signing an incorrect bill.
    For an indistinct bill.
    For an incorrect address.
    Any assistant shall be fined 6d.
12. Talking, laughing, or congregating together in departments – fine 6d.
13. Any assistant being ill must at once have the doctor sent for, and any assistant being ill or not at business on Monday morning will be fined three days' pay unless the doctor certifies that they are unfit for business.

'Living-in'

As shops were organized at this time, they could either provide secure, life-long employment, offering the opportunity to learn real skills and to work one's way up the ladder to a position of authority, or else they could impose tyranny and fear, and exploit their workers for little financial reward. These differences were highlighted in the aspect of 'living-in'. For a long time, it had been customary for the small independent shop to provide living accommodation for its workers, or apprentices (usually males), and with the coming of larger stores and multiples, this system continued and was in full operation until the First World War. Assistants were often compelled to live in quarters on the shop premises or in hostels close by. Their food was provided, and their behaviour in their free time governed by rules as to when they must be in at night, what they were allowed to keep in their rooms, and so on. At the better stores, assistants were well fed and looked after in what was almost a family atmosphere, as Leonard Thoday of Heal's recalls:

I was amazed at the quantity and quality of the food prepared by the housekeeper. For breakfast there was usually a ham from which we ourselves carved as much as we could eat, with bread and butter, marmalade or jam and tea. Lunch was served in two parties and consisted of a joint with vegetables and sweet.

At other premises, experiences of living-in were horrific. When P.C. Hoffman came to London as a boy in 1894 and began work as a draper's assistant, he suffered extreme misery through living-in.

I found myself along with half-a-dozen other young shavers in a small dirty room with six beds packed very close together.... Both walls and ceilings were bare, grimy and splotched. The two windows, being curtained with dirt, needed no other obscuring. The naked gas jet had a wire cage over it.... The gas was turned out at the main at 11.15. One of the boys lighted a piece of candle and they hunted for bugs on the wall, cracking them with slipper heels. They stuffed cracks in the wall with soap.... I thought my sensitive heart would break. I sobbed through that dismal night. (*They Also Serve*)

Rules often included obligatory attendance at church on Sundays, and forbade assistants to be in their rooms at all during daylight hours on their day off. Sometimes they could be fined for bringing flowers or pictures into their bedrooms, or other such petty infringements of the rules.

Fire risks were high in these lodging quarters, and employers often ignored any legal requirements to take safety precautions. In 1912, five girls died at John Barker's in Kensington, when fire swept through their living area. Some of the more militant shop-workers began to protest about compulsory living-in and the standards of food and accommodation that they were expected to put up with, but, in fact, it was the outbreak of war which really put an end to the system, since

---

12 *A bill of 1880 shows how carefully the assistant had to enter and add up the purchases made by each customer.*

employers could not find staff so easily, nor provide meals for them due to food shortages. Although some shops carried on providing hostel accommodation for their employees right up until the 1970s, this has been on a voluntary basis, and, of course, with proper food and facilities provided. 'Living-in' continued as a service to the assistants, rather than as a way of keeping them available to work long hours and of providing extra profit for the shop from the rent they charged.

Women in shops

In late Victorian and Edwardian times, more and more women were going into shop work. Earlier in the nineteenth century, very few, apart from those who ran their own village store, were found as shop assistants. Retail shops themselves were growing in number, and it is estimated that whereas in 1875 there were 295,000 shops in the U.K., by 1907 there were 459,592. More factory goods and a relative rise in personal income, plus better transport by rail, meant that shops could obtain and sell more goods. Because women were generally paid lower wages than their male counterparts, employers started to look to women to fill vacancies in their expanding businesses. Many customers appreciated being served by women:

Women are so much quicker than men, and they understand so much more readily what other women want; they can enter into the little troubles of their customer. (Lady Jeune in the *Fortnightly Review*, 1896)

Female assistants looked to marriage rather than to a career, however, as their eventual hope of security. It was common to be sacked if business was slack, and difficult for women over 30 to find another job. Additionally, the strain of long hours on their feet often caused ill health and forced women to leave their jobs sooner than they had intended. Most shops were still male-dominated, and women had little chance of attaining a high position, although in Marks and Spencer's in the early years of this century one could find a manageress in charge of a team of ten or more assistants.

At the other extreme of shop life, women could be found running their own businesses from home, where they might open when they liked, and sell what they pleased to whom they pleased. Margaret Penn, growing up in the Lancashire village of Hollins Green around 1909, remembers:

The chief centre of interest in The Street was Mrs Amelia Starkey's general shop. Mrs Starkey was short, fat, dark, quick-tempered but good-natured, and she sold everything from paraffin oil to black treacle and jewel-studded back combs. Every child in the village always went willingly on an errand to Amelia Starkey's, for she never failed to give each one a sweet ... Besides Mrs Starkey's big shop, there was Fanny Wright's parlour shop, where for one penny you could buy a whole quarter of a pound of American gums, and where also it was possible to get a ha'porth or even a penn'orth of sweets on credit. But Mrs Wright only allowed such generous terms to trusted customers, and then only to make sure of getting their regular Saturday trade, for her rival, Mrs Starkey, never allowed credit to any but grownups. Mrs Wright's was known as 'the parlour-shop' because she had simply turned her front room into a shop, and she only sold sweets and, on Saturday nights, fish and chips. (*Manchester Fourteen Miles*)

2 War and Peace: 1914-30

In 1926 a writer in the magazine *Country Life* commented:

Mrs Hunneybun's village shop . . . you can still remember, it may be, the mingled smells of that delightful shop; the sweetness of apples drying in a large bin, the perfume of coltsfoot rock, the faint aromatic background of clove and allspice. You remember, too, the dim light that filtered into the shop-parlour through the leaded green panes of the casement window, and you have not forgotten the excellent value of Mrs Hunneybun's merchandise . . . . But round the corner, long ago, began to grow up horrors of glaring red brick and galvanized iron, places which used methods far different from Mrs Hunneybun's peaceful persuasion, and whose appearance corresponded with the qualities of their contents and the morals of their owners. Since then things have gone from bad to worse. Our villages have been invaded by the great multiple shops from the cities, controlled and managed by the 'foreigners' with no interests in the neighbourhood or knowledge of people.

Although this is an exaggerated and rather sentimental view, it does reflect the growing presence of multiple stores, especially grocery and clothing firms, after the First World War, and the growth of a suburban way of life, aided by car and bus transport, which was taking over from the old pattern of village shopping. What the writer conveniently chooses to forget is that the Mrs Hunneybuns were often temperamental, unhygienic, and erratic in their opening hours, whereas the new-style shops of the 1920s were usually spacious, clean, well-lit, with the goods of a more reliable quality.

Wartime changes

It was the war itself which accelerated changes. Immediately it broke out in 1914, thousands of men and boys volunteered for the armed forces, and by its end in 1918, over five million had taken part in military service. Some shops, fired by the patriotic spirit of the times, kept their former male workers on full pay while they were in the army or navy. This was a very welcome measure, since men in the forces were scarcely paid enough to keep their families fed and housed.

There was an acute shortage of labour, with so many men away fighting. Women came forward to fill many of the vacancies, and for the first time women of the higher social classes found themselves serving customers, dusting displays and taking money at the cash desk. Many well-bred young ladies, such as Marguerite Cardell, who helped a butcher with his delivery round, looked on the work as a welcome break from the closely chaperoned life of Edwardian society:

At present my employer is unable to find work enough for me all day, but as time passes . . . the care of the horse may fall to me. This will mean earlier hours and more work altogether. Yet it will be delightful work, for nothing is more interesting to one than the care of the horse one drives daily, and which is associated with all one's work in all weathers.' (Quoted in *Women War Workers* by Gilbert Stone, 1917)

On some occasions, the grandest ladies of them all would help out in a store on a voluntary basis, as in Brown and Chester's, where a sale was held in 1915, half the takings of which were given to the local War Relief Fund:

The ordinary customer becoming the purchaser of a bewitching gown or a dream of a hat could easily have had the great honour of being assisted in her choice by . . . a Duchess or a Marchioness. (H.D. Willcock [ed.], *Brown and Chester*)

Although many women returned to domestic life after the war, large numbers, having enjoyed their employment and the attraction of a regular wage, stayed on at work. Stores such as Barker's of Kensington tried to expand their business so that they could keep on both their wartime female employees and provide jobs again for the men returning from the forces.

Restrictions and rationing

During the First World War, the Government imposed various restrictions on life in Britain to try and conserve resources and goods in a way never before known, and shops were allowed to open only for a certain number of hours. Although bread, meat, sugar and other foodstuffs were not properly rationed until 1918, raw materials and factory production were controlled, which meant that shops had difficulty in stocking all the goods they had sold previously. Small groceries, greengroceries and butchers', shops had to cope with queues forming, and devise ways of sharing out foodstuffs which were in short supply. Some kept amounts back for their favourite customers, while others sold scarce items, such as sugar, only to those who were willing to buy other goods at the same time. The introduction in 1918 of rationing meant that food could be shared out in a fairer manner, but it was a very wearying procedure for both the shopkeeper and the customer:

I have vivid memories of waiting in a butcher's shop standing in a queue of about twenty other women. I wondered what I should be able to secure for my three meat coupons. I had set my heart on a piece of silverside. I was the eighteenth in the queue . . . . The butcher, a quick and clever surgeon, chopped off all sorts of nice-looking little joints for which I yearned . . . But after twenty joints had been carved . . . there seemed but little chance of my obtaining silverside. I approached the butcher furtively. 'Have you any silverside?' I whispered. 'No, no silverside – breast, scrag or bit o'brisket,' he yapped at me impatiently . . . . I gasped 'Brisket', and then found myself on the pavement clasping lovingly a very minute parcel of stringy meat. (Mrs C.S. Peel, *How We Lived Then*, 1929)

Belgian refugees

A new generation of shopkeepers who began business during the war were the Belgian refugees who came to Britain in their thousands after German troops had invaded their native land. At first housed in halls and hostels, they later began to integrate into the community and many of them set up in business. They achieved a reputation for being excellent pastry-cooks and confectioners.

Air-raid precautions

Britain itself was never invaded, but the Germans did carry out air-raids, which killed over 1000 people during the course of the war, chiefly in London and in coastal towns. The attacks were on nothing like the scale experienced in the Second World War, but, nevertheless, shops in London sometimes had to take precautions by sending staff and customers to the basement while the air-raid alarms sounded.

Post-war 'emporiums'

In the years after the war, a desire for modernity in shops competed with the old and cherished notions of leisure and luxury. Department stores and large 'emporiums' had been founded, as we have seen, on the notion of palatial splendour and

13 Department stores tried to provide facilities for their customers similar to those they might find in a hotel or exclusive club – here, a ladies' 'rest room' for reading and writing in Glasgow, 1924.

elegance. For the time being, this continued, and was indeed welcomed after the hardships and shortages of the war. Stores such as Liberty's had 'cicerones' or commissionaires standing at the door to greet each customer as he or she arrived, and to conduct him or her to the appropriate department. 'I was met at the doorway by a gray-haired, alert, beautifully gowned lady, smiling and gracious as a princess,' recalled one American customer of the times. Superb rest rooms and coffee lounges were provided by some department stores for their customers, giving the atmosphere more of an exclusive club than of a commercial enterprise. And the assistants were still expected to defer to these customers on all occasions. The *Rules Book* of Brown and Muff, Bradford, 1925, stated severely that 'complaints by Customers of incivility or inattention' would be thoroughly investigated.

Where it is proved that any Member of Staff has wilfully given offence to any Customer from any cause whatever, such employee will be subject to instant dismissal.

This meant that staff still felt insecure; a misunderstanding, or deliberate provocation by an awkward customer could lead instantly to the end of their career.

Early union action

Some shop-workers were anxious to establish better rights and conditions for themselves. The

The SPIRIT of the HOUSE

To look upon each minute as precious and to be exchanged only for its full equivalent in Progress... To develop, continually, every faculty which helps to build greater judgment, energy, determination, imagination, mirth and good cheer, for each is necessary to the strong happy individual... To look upon Work during the working hours of the day as a privilege—as a game—as a requisite of the full and complete life... To look upon Idleness with disrespect, as a waste of Time, the only commodity of which everyone has an equal amount... To feel that the waking hours after the day's work is over, are best used in study, in agreeable companionship, in recreation, in those acts which build happier, stronger character and better health... To strive for higher Standards and Ideals... To look upon the bright side of things and be Optimists in the best meaning of the word... To act quickly and avoid procrastination... To think always Broad-mindedly and to scorn Narrow-mindedness, Meanness and Jealousy... To be Just and to despise Injustice... To punish Dishonesty with the utmost effort... To appreciate fully Intelligence, Originality, Loyalty—recognising merit and merit only as the door to advancement... To acknowledge no obstacles as insurmountable which stand in the way of splendid Progress.

14 *How Selfridge's staff were encouraged to be thoroughly dedicated to their work in 1920*

---

first proper trade union to which they could belong had been formed in 1891. This was called the National Union of Shop Assistants, later renamed the National Amalgamated Union of Shop Assistants, Warehousemen and Clerks, and was founded by 17 representatives of local shop assistants' associations. To begin with, assistants had not been keen to join. They had considered their position too 'respectable' and superior to that of labourers and manual workers, who formed the core of the union's membership. But numbes had gradually increased: by 1910 there were 22,426 members but, by 1914, there were 81,250, over a quarter of whom were women. In their early days, the unions were responsible more for bringing exploitation and poor working conditions to the attention of the public and the Government than for achieving legislation; it was the war which really secured shorter working hours, and put an end to compulsory 'living-in'. Even in the 1920s, however, many assistants kept clear of the unions and actively opposed any militant action. A considerable number of staff at John Lewis's, Oxford Street, London, refused to have anything to do with a strike called by the union on the day of the 'Silk Sale' in 1920. Mrs A. Razzell recalls:

When I and other non-strikers arrived at the Staff entrance on Monday morning we were greeted with boos, which, needless to say, did not worry us.... After the first day or two of the strike some of the strikers began to return to work. After a few days, those still on strike were informed that unless they returned by a specified date their engagement would be closed. This, of course, brought more back but fortunately none of the agitators returned. (*John Lewis Gazette*, 1959)

The American influence

In the post-war period, owners and managers of large stores began to look to America for new ideas of layout, equipment and staffing. Trevor Bowen, chairman of Barker's, in Kensington, made 12 visits to the USA between 1919 and 1950, and after his very first visit returned with the novel idea that staff should be encouraged to enjoy themselves out of hours! A sports club was then established, where all kinds of team and athletic events could take place, and dances and whist drives were held in the pavilion. Employers were coming to realize that their workers could be more cheerful, energetic and willing if they were given the opportunities for recreation and social occasions, and that a good spirit of co-operation could be established this way. The old notion of the boss as dictator still prevailed, but it was being tempered by the idea of a benevolent father figure whose 'family' of staff supported him willingly and affectionately. The head of Bentall's

15 A trip to Malvern enjoyed by staff of Howell's, Cardiff in 1925. The 'charabanc' they are riding in was an early form of motor coach.

16 A tailor's shop. Many stores still employed tailors and seamstresses to produce 'made to measure' clothes, especially suits and coats, for customers.

17 New, clean and bright lines were emerging in shop layouts, ideas which managers often borrowed from American practice. This is a grocery department at John Lewis's in Welwyn Garden City in 1922.

store, in Kingston-upon-Thames, Surrey, valued 'team spirit and loyalty', and wrote in his staff book for the 1920s: 'I want each one to get the Big Idea of Bentall's as an entity.'

Nevertheless, he and others still upheld strict rules of conduct for staff on duty. It was considered improper at Bentall's for an assistant to leave the store at lunchtime without a hat, and if one wished to marry, he or she had formally to ask the staff manager for permission. At Brown and Muff's the management had the 'Right of Search' to check any assistant at any time to see that nothing had been stolen, and a timekeeper was kept on duty at the staff entrance 'to prevent loitering, undue commotion, or any other irregularity'.

Irregular practice

Irregularity of practice in serving customers was certainly well-known, and had been for many years, despite the assertion of the writer at the beginning of the chapter that the era of 'Mrs Hunneybun' had been one of perfect morality. A young salesman, Mr H.M. Tobias, starting his career in a provisions shop in 1923, was taught how to tip the scales, to give short change, and to beat extra water into the butter! He was also instructed to put false labels on wine bottles and to hide in poor pieces of meat with the good ones. There was a particular form of slang which the assistants used to avoid detection; by saying words backwards they could warn each other that a customer was 'Toh no Elacs', for instance, when it come to weighing up.

Sharp practices were not regarded as dishonest then. It was the accepted practice in the food trade. (*John Lewis Gazette*, 1974).

18 *A haberdasher's shop, 1930. Note the number of drawers and shelves that the assistants had to be familiar with, and the fact that customers could sit down to be served.*

19 *A hat shop; the millinery business was thought suitable for upper-class ladies.*

Opportunities for those 'of gentle birth'

And although certain forms of village and family trade were dying out, others were growing. The involvement of higher-class women in shop work during the war meant that in the 1920s it had now become acceptable for 'ladies' to run a small shop or business, provided that the trade was not too 'inferior' in its nature. Tea-rooms, lingerie and haberdashery were all considered suitable occupations for single ladies or for those who had fallen upon difficult times after the war.

Advertisements placed in *The Lady* in July 1921 offered opportunities to those 'of gentle birth' and with the 'highest social and business references':

Lady having small capital wishes to meet lady with same, view to partnership, tea-rooms or light business.

Lady, trained sweet and chocolate-making . . . requires post in tea-room or confectionery business run by gentlewoman.

Even though the refinement and delicacy of all this may strike us as being amusing and somewhat absurd today, the First World War had, nevertheless, opened up the way for women of all classes and status to take their place in shop-keeping, and to work as owners and managers, rather than as employed assistants.

20 *A 'genteel' tea-room in an Edinburgh store, 1924. A later photograph from the 1950s shows that the uniform remained unchanged for 30 years!*

3 The 1930s: Science in Selling

The moves made in the 1920s to up-date sales methods and staff policy began to bear fruit in the 1930s. 'Scientific' methods were becoming popular in various areas of life; there were 'scientific' ways of slimming, keeping fit, processing food, or doing housework, for instance, which were all associated with a drive towards efficiency, economy and hygiene.

The same interest in science and efficiency can be found, too, in the world of retailing at this time. Books were published telling managers how to improve the training of their staff and spurring on the assistants themselves to greater efforts:

The science of salesmanship is most important, in view of the competition... today, and no matter how good the sales staff is, a course of salesmanship will result in keener interest and in every single individual making greater efforts to carry each enquiry to its proper finale – a sale.

The five phases to which reference has been made are:
1 Awakening Attention.
2 Stimulating Interest.
3 Creating the Desire to Possess.
4 Forming the Resolve to Buy.
5 Deciding to Place the Order.

... The art of salesmanship consists of arresting the Attention, then guiding the customer's mind through the Interest phase, creating Desire, helping to form the Resolve to buy and finally booking the Order; and, once the order is placed, to convey the impression that the Decision is a wise one which will never be regretted. (W.A. Gibson Martin, *The Furnishing Soft Goods Department*, 1930)

21 *A* Punch *cartoon from 1932 showing the kind of sales gimmicks used to persuade customers to buy up 'bargain' offers*

Wife (*emerging delightedly from shop*). "LOOK WHAT THEY GAVE ME FOR SPENDING TWO POUNDS!"

Staff training

The competition for custom which is mentioned was indeed fierce at this time, since for most of the 1930s Britain was in the grip of an economic depression. By training their staff intensively, and promoting goods more openly through window displays, special offers and so on, many shops hoped to hold out against the fall-off in trade. Firms such as Cadbury's, the confectioners, tried to help out and to boost their own sales by sending round representatives with display material for shop windows and by opening an advice bureau, which shopkeepers could consult to find out the best way of offering their goods to the public.

Multiple stores began to set up training schools in order to make their assistants more knowledgeable and encourage them to sell more actively. At the United Dairies, for instance, trainees would learn about milk processing, testing and bottling as well as attending lectures.

At the end of an assistant's course ... a report is made by the head of the school to the district manager, scoring his work under salesmanship, service and window display. (A.E. Hammond, *Multiple Shop Organization*, 1930).

Rather than keep a respectable gap between the work of the sales assistant and that of factory production, as had been the tradition, the new outlook was to interest the shop staff in the production of the goods they sold. Woolworth's stores had a policy of arranging visits to factories for their assistants, which, judging by the many letters included in the house magazine *The New Bond*, they enjoyed very much as a day out:

We gazed in wonder at the intricate machinery that cut tinfoil into squares and wrapped the chocolates; at the yards and yards of sweetness that went into one end of the machine and came out the other as Mint Lumps. Each room held a new surprise. Watching the girls box-making proved most interesting, as did seeing the twopenny bags of boiled sweets, so familiar to Woolworth employees, being weighed, placed in bags and tied.

The effect of the recession

Not all such efforts were successful, however, in coping with the economic recession, and sometimes stores had to make their staff redundant or reduce their wages. In 1931, Brown and Muff's announced:

We regret that the trend of events has necessitated a general review of wages of the Staff, many of which have been reduced.... We wish to assure you that the reductions which have had to be made are extremely distasteful to us.

In the poorer city areas, small shops struggled to keep going. In 1932 Cadbury's carried out a survey of sweet shops and found that many had a turnover of £10 or less a week, whereas a

22 *A team of staff from a Woolworth's store in a keep-fit display, reflecting the 1930s fashion for health and fitness*

minimum of £20 was needed for shopkeeper to make even a modest living.

It would be going too far to say that the continued existence of all such shops is against the public interest, though this is undoubtedly true of those which are badly run and unhygienic.

Pawnbrokers', where customers could obtain money for their own possessions, and then 'redeem' them later at a higher price if they could afford it, flourished. Mrs Leah North, who started her career in retailing as a pawnbroker's assistant, recalls:

One woman used to pawn her husband's suit every week, then buy it back again so that he had it to wear on Sundays.

Improving efficiency

In the larger stores new equipment was brought in in the drive for efficiency and to keep custom. John Lewis's, for instance, finally decided to adopt cash registers, after asking their 'Intelligence Department' to carry out a survey to prove that they really would save time. Previously, sales had been conducted in a very tedious way, whereby the assistant, the supervisor and the cashier might all be involved in a transaction, with the bills being written out by hand. Bentall's department store took the radical step of installing escalators in their store to attract customers. These were quite a novelty in Britain at that period, and when they first came into operation the 1000 sales staff were lined up, given meticulous instructions on how to use them, and then made to ride solemnly up and down till they were confident of where to put their feet!

23 *A lively window display in a hardware store in Hexham, Co. Durham*

Marks and Spencer's, working on American lines, redesigned many of their shops so that they could be lighter and brighter, with large plate glass windows and better displays, including 'island counters' which the public could walk round. They, like other retail firms, did a good deal for their employees' welfare at this time, by, for instance, providing canteens, rest-rooms, and sickness benefits. In earlier years, shops had often offered no sickness pay, or had left it up to the whim of the employer to provide money to help out the family of an ailing assistant.

Improving customer appeal

Certain of the larger stores also tried to keep up their customer appeal by introducing various exotic attractions. Barker's of Kensington opened a roof garden, with Spanish, Tudor and English

24 *The arrival of radio in the 1930s opened up a new line of business for the retail trade.*

25 *A shoe shop from Minehead, Somerset, promotes its wares with a display at a local exhibition, staffed by two of the shop's assistants.*

water-garden areas, palm trees, fountains and wrought-iron balconies. Brown and Chester's put on archaeological exhibitions, fashion parades, and tea-dances. Bentall's went even further, with a lady diving 60 foot from the top floor into a pool on the ground floor! They also brought an entire circus into the building at Christmas. This caused problems for the staff, since some of them had to walk past the lions' cages on their way home and others, on one occasion, had to pursue two escaped monkeys, who were finally discovered smashing bottles in the wine store. Novel displays like these would have been thought vulgar by the Edwardian staff of such prestigious stores, but in the 1930s they helped to create an illusion of glamour and a welcome contrast to the hardship and depression that the country was experiencing.

26 *One of the updated Marks and Spencer stores of the 1930s; this one is at Leicester.*

Social events

Social and sporting activities for staff were in full

swing in the 1930s. Often stores would organize annual outings, such as this one to Blackpool for the staff of Woolworth's in Sale:

We had a wonderful time. The weather was fine and everyone was full of 'beans'. All the younger girls spent their time on the Pleasure Beach and then turned up for tea looking rather sick, but that did not seem to affect their appetites. The rest of us hired a landau and drove around Blackpool feeling like the 'Idle Rich' . . . . After tea we went to view the lights, which were very fine, and then returned home after a jolly good day. (*The New Bond*, January 1938).

In the evenings, assistants in department or multiple stores could join in keep-fit classes, rehearsals for musical shows or drama societies. A review in a local paper of *The Chinese Puzzle*, a play presented by staff from Chiesman's Lewisham, shows how well such productions were supported:

The play seemed to give infinite delight to the audience. From another point of view . . . I wished that the infinity of applause had been somewhat more discriminating, for there was an aggravating round of clapping at nearly every important exit. Obviously the Players had many friends beyond the footlights who were over-keen to appreciate their sterling efforts for a worthy cause. (*Lewisham Journal*, March 1935)

Old customs, new technology

In this period, as at all times, some shops were far more up-to-date in their methods than others. Assistants in many butchers' or fishmongers', for instance, still had to drag in blocks of ice as they were delivered to keep the food fresh, since

27 *A delivery boy from a butcher's shop. The butcher boy bike, with its front basket set to carry large packages, was a familiar sight in the 1930s and 1940s.*

refrigeration was not in general use. Deliveries of goods from the shop to the customer were often carried out by horse and cart, although some stores had had motor vans since the First World War. Michael Deering, who now runs a village sub-post office and general stores, recalls his childhood in the 1930s:

All the tradesmen called, even with the minutest items. The egg man used to come once a fortnight in a gig with a small pony on the front. He wore his best suit and bowler hat – he always had a brown suit, which never seemed to match the hat! He had a big wicker basket of eggs and he would bring them round for you to choose the eggs yourself, as many as you wanted.

Telephones, if installed at all, were treated gingerly and with awe: 'A call put through to London was a real event – something you told your family about when you got home in the evening' remembers Peggy Marchant, who worked in the Counting House at Knight and Lee's, Southsea.

Changing attitudes

Overall, at this time there was a move to give staff more responsibility, to train them better, and to encourage them to express their views. *Selfridge's Guide Book* of the 1930s makes mention of 'suggestions boxes' which were placed around the store:

It is hoped that the Staff will make liberal use of this method of expressing their opinions of

28 *Heal's furniture store was still using a horse-drawn van for some of their deliveries.*

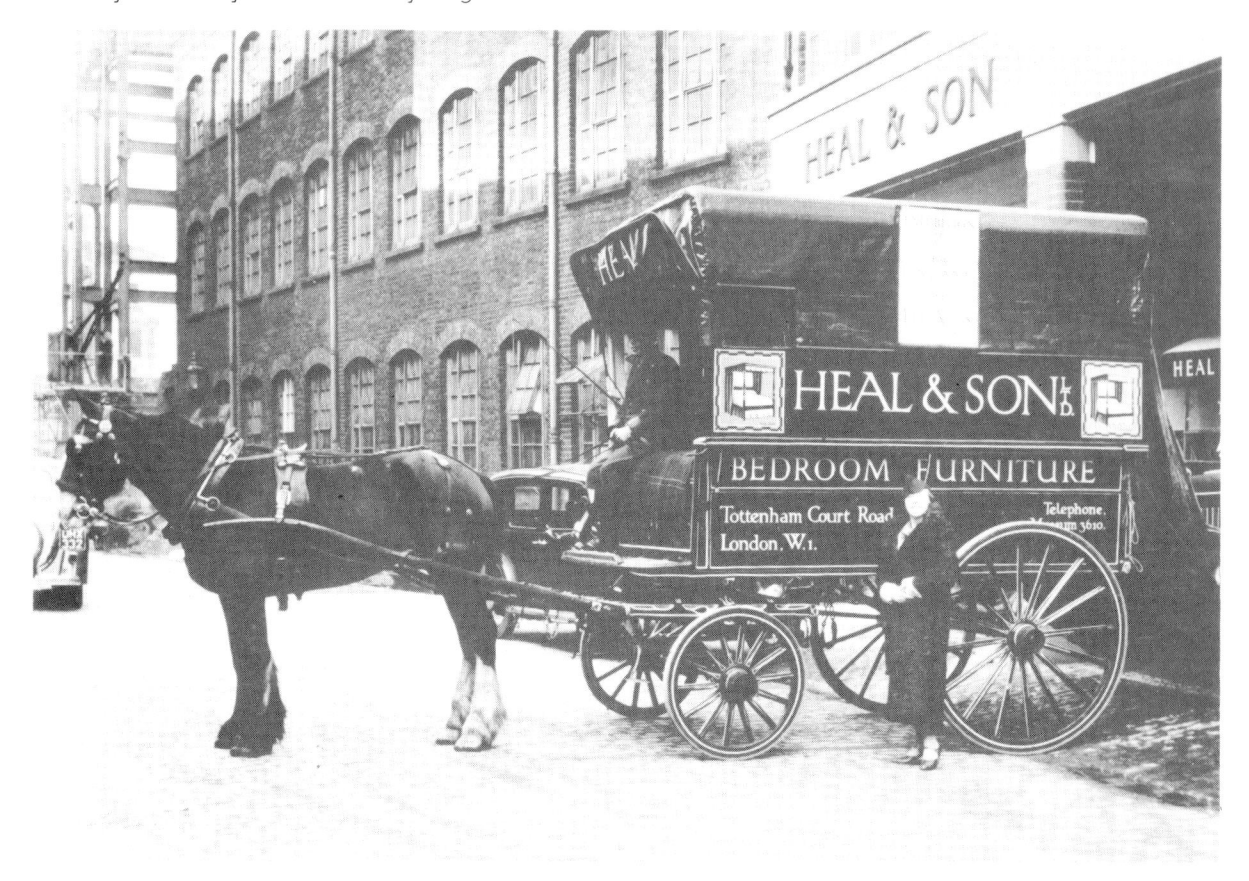

> ### RECEIPT FOR GUIDE BOOK.
>
> *I hereby acknowledge to have received a copy of the Guide Book of this establishment which I promise to carefully read and study to enable me to carry out intelligently the Rules, Regulations and Policies of the House of Selfridge.*
>
> *I further promise to return this Book on leaving the employment of Selfridge & Co. Ltd.*
>
> *(Sig.)*

29 *A page from the* Selfridge's Staff Guide Book *of the 1930s*

everything concerning the welfare of the business.

The same booklet also shows that the relationship between assistants and customers was changing, and that the assistants, while still expected always to remain polite, could take a pride in their own position and work:

Treat visitors neither with familiarity, nor servility, but always with dignity and true courtesy.

In many ways, the 1930s can be seen as one of the happiest decades of shop work. Although the years were hard economically and there was much poverty in Britain, for those who had jobs life could be very rewarding. In shops, many of the old skills were still employed: – grocers, for instance, still learnt how to choose and blend teas, how to weight up butter from tubs and cut cheeses, and clothing assistants would still measure customers and advise on style, material and alterations. Assistants often came into a business intending to make it a lifetime's career, and could hope to work their way right up the ladder to managerial positions through experience and commitment. (Later it became more common for graduates and specially recruited trainees to be taken straight into management.) And, with a relaxing of the old Victorian rules on conduct and manner, staff were perhaps freer to enjoy working together as a team, as the amount of time spent together out of hours in social events shows.

4 Wartime and the Post-War Period

When Britain went to war with Germany in 1939, the pattern of life was severely disrupted. Several million British citizens, both men and women, joined the armed forces. Over 270,000 of them were killed, and more than 60,000 civilians were killed in German bombing raids. The raids destroyed large parts of cities such as London, Bristol and Coventry, making travelling and shopping a hazardous business. Supplies of goods became scarce; the Government stepped

---

30 *Heal's Home Guard being put through their paces on the shop's rooftop*

in to control their manufacture, and also to ration essential fuel, food and clothing.

31 An assistant helping soldiers to choose Valentine cards for their sweethearts

Conscription

All these events, of course, affected the running of shops. First of all, a large proportion of shop staff, from counter hands to managers, left to go into the army, navy or air force. Some shops formed their own companies of soldiers. In certain shops, indeed, these had been operating on a voluntary basis for a number of years, as a precaution against the build up of military power in Germany and the threat of war. At other stores, such as Barker's of Kensington, a 'battery' of volunteer soldiers had been formed in 1925 as part of the general staff activities. Before the war broke out, their duties had consisted mainly of a fortnight's training by the sea each year, for which they were given extra pay and holidays! However, during the war years this became a serious full-time occupation; they worked first on gun sites in

32 *Some shops helped the war effort by putting on special displays, such as this one, in which the public is encouraged to invest their money in Defence Bonds.*

London, and were then sent out to Kenya on active service.

Shop staff were encouraged to support their fellow workers in the armed forces. Employees of Harrods' sent parcels containing cigarettes, woollen clothes and books to cheer up the troops serving abroad. The store's own magazine, *The Gazette*, kept soldiers in touch with life at home, and helped to provide them with a few extra comforts:

Only last month we put a request in the Gazette for a radio for one of our lads serving on a minesweeper, and the next day one of our staff very kindly brought along a portable radio – free of charge. (*Harrod's Scrapbook*)

It was not only the male staff who were conscripted into the army; from 1941 women could also be called up for war-work or to serve in the women's armed forces. By 1943 the age-range for women's conscription was 18 to 50. This led to staffing shortages (figures for one department store reveal that by 1942 83 per cent of the total staff had left for war-work) and problems with employees coming and going.

The 1941 Chairman's Report at Brown and Chester stated:

We have had a turnover of staff . . . far in excess of anything we could possibly welcome. Far too much time has been spent during the year in training and retraining people to our work in our way.

Wartime staff changes

The shortage of men, however, was greater than that of women, which meant that women were able to take over some of the managerial positions previously reserved for male staff. They also moved into other occupations normally filled by men, such as driving delivery vans. Delivery services had, in any case, to be cut down, as fuel was scarce; (Bentall's of Kingston tried using motorbikes with sidecars for small orders, but found that this did tend to shake the icing off

33 A.R.P. (Air Raid Patrol) wardens at Brown and Muff's, Bradford. These members of staff had been trained to deal with bombing raid emergencies.

37

34 *Some stores gave over part of their floor space to war work; here we see the parachute factory at Heal's, in Tottenham Court Road, London.*

cakes!) People of all ages came in to fill the vacancies in shops, including retired people aged 80 or over who helped out where they could. Many nurseries were set up for the first time, to make it easier for women with young children to go to work.

The general shake-up of shop organization eased the strict order of relationships between the different grades of staff. Those shops which had formed volunteer batallions just before the war had already experienced this to some degree, since the military ranks in these by no means corresponded to the hierarchy in the shop, and during army manoeuvres a senior manager could find himself under orders from a humble salesman! War brought a more tolerant and flexible attitude into shop work; when Leah

North worked part-time on a biscuit counter at a department store she was amazed, on one occasion, to escape retribution:

The department manager came round one day when I had just stuffed my mouth full of biscuits, and asked me a question. I looked up at him, absolutely flummoxed! He just said, 'I'll call back later, when your mouth's empty.'

Air-raids and their effect on shopping

War, however, brought danger too. Shopping centres were under threat of attack from German bombing raids. The major stores took precautions by training their staff to deal with fires, evacuation procedures and first-aid. At first, the attitude was often casual, and when air-raid warnings sounded staff might simply close the shop doors and leave those inside to dive under counters or desks. But as the intensity of bombing increased during the war, shelters were built in the basement, and were often used by other people in the locality as well as those already in the store. Marks and Spencer's not only allowed their air-raid shelters to be used, but helped to provide food for those who had been made homeless.

Many shops were destroyed by bombs, and some managed to carry on business by setting up

---

35 *After Bond's store, Norwich, was destroyed in 1942, staff tried to keep going by selling goods from buses standing in a nearby car park.*

mobile sales vans or erecting 'pre-fab' huts on the bombed site until they could begin rebuilding. Even those which remained standing might suffer broken windows from the effects of a nearby blast. The raids could have their humorous side too – when there was a direct hit on a London dental firm, countless pairs of false teeth were propelled through the windows of the Counting House at Liberty's!

Staff had to take it in turns to do fire-watching duty at night, to spot and extinguish any fires that might arise on their own or nearby premises.

Some department stores were able to provide temporary homes for staff whose own homes had been damaged, or for whom it was too dangerous to travel back at the end of the day. At Barker's, Kensington, employees remembered with affection the sociable nights they had spent in the shelters, with amusements such as piano and snooker playing. The managing director, himself made homeless by enemy action, set up his office and living quarters in the basement for several months. Barkers were well-organized by day, too, with 200 staff on duty ready to close the store and help customers reach the shelter when the sirens sounded. After the first year or so of the war, the bomb alerts could last for hours at a time, cutting down drastically shop opening hours. Trade in city centres suffered very badly, since customers were wary of travelling far from their homes, and being caught in air-raids. Many preferred to use small local shops, or visit suburban high streets which they could reach quickly.

36 *Gamage's department store of London was partially destroyed by bombing.*

Rationing

In addition, when rationing was introduced in January 1940, customers had to restrict the number of shops they visited. Coupons were needed to buy food such as meat, tea and sugar, and a family had to register with a particular retail supplier. Food in general was in short supply, and it was a headache for the shopkeepers to distribute it fairly. Some shops, like Harrods, tried to keep their regular customers happy. In the bakery department a quarter of the cakes were kept back for them, and they were told to come to the counter after the first queues had dispersed.

Judgement as to who is thus served is left in the hands of three assistants who know the customers well.

However, in the fish department, Mr Fleming's practice of 'looking after' his favourite regular shoppers was condemned as 'dubious' by the management, who also commented that complaints were coming in from customers that the best fish was saved for those who ordered by phone – these would probably have been the well-to-do customers with credit accounts at the store.

It was not unknown for some shopkeepers to fiddle the rationing system and make illegal profits by letting customers have extra food for higher prices. Sainsbury's, on the other hand, decided to make an advertising campaign out of their attitude towards honest dealing, and in 1945 adopted the slogan, 'The things you see rarely are all shared out fairly'.

PAINTS   COLOURS   GLASS

W. E. TAYLOR & SON

Telephone 54454

Telegrams :
" Taylor,
Colour Merchant,
Exeter "

BUILDERS' AND PLUMBERS' MERCHANTS

ROUGEMONT PRODUCTS

150 FORE STREET, EXETER
(And Friernhay Street)

May. 22nd. 1946.

Dear Mr Shepherd.
    Many thanks for your letter order received this morning but we regret that we are entirely out of stock of all the items you require. We only have knotting in stock in half gallons and Sunray Distemper only arrives once a month and then only lasts about two days, leaving us out of stock for 28 days a month.
    We are very sorry that this is the position but feel sure you will understand the present difficulties of the demand by far exceeding the supply.
    Perhaps you will make a stock order in quantities, to keep you going whilst we are waiting for our monthly quotas, if you would do this we will do our utmost to send all your order when our quota arrives,.
    Yours Faithfully,

Mr S.G.Shepherd,
  Oldways End,
    East Anstey,
      N.Devon,.

per pro W. E. TAYLOR & SON,
150 FORE ST., EXETER.

The Government took over control of the manufacturing and sale of goods, to conserve materials and supplies, since very little could be brought into the country by boat during the war, and many raw materials such as wool and metal were needed to make ammunition, equipment and uniforms for the armed forces. From 1941 clothes rationing was in force, and under the 'Utility' scheme both clothing and furniture had to be made in accordance with Government standards, so that economical and essential products were marketed rather than luxury goods.

Dealing with coupons was yet another technique that sales assistants had to learn:

Coupons are clipped from the customer's Ration Book by the Buyer, Assistant Buyer, or Buyer's Clerk only, after initialling the sales bill to which they refer, and entering the number of coupons on it. They are then placed in a locked metal box. (*Harrods Scrapbook*)

The turnover of many shops fell sharply during the war, since they could not buy in the quantity of goods that they wanted. Peter Hewith, an assistant at Heal's furniture shop, remembered a customer coming in and showing interest in every carpet in the showroom:

I thought, 'This is marvellous' because I was on a commission.... 'I'm doing very well.' And then it appeared that.... he was another retailer. Supplies were so bad that he was prepared to pay our prices. (Quoted in *Where We Used to Work* by Kenneth Hudson and John Baker.)

Unfortunately for Peter Hewitt, he was not allowed to sell the shop's stock in this way!

After the war ended in 1945, rationing still continued for several years until supplies got back to normal again. Shopkeepers were faced with the tedious job of writing to different manufacturers in the hope of tracking down the goods that they wanted to stock. Even if they could find a consignment on offer, transport was not always available, as this letter, dated 27 March 1947, shows:

Dear Sir/s,
    An embargo has been placed by the Railway Authorities on goods to be delivered in your area. Consequently the parcel of lighter fuel has not been despatched by us. As soon as this embargo is lifted, your order will have our immediate attention.
Robert Sinclair
Tobacco Co Ltd

And when luxury goods were manufactured once more, they were frequently creamed off for export sales in order to help boost the national economy and speed up the post-war recovery.

Post-war developments

For many working women, the end of the Second World War, unlike that of the First, did not mean the end of their jobs. In the food retail trade, for instance, women had come to outnumber male employees during the war, and the balance has remained this way ever since. Many women who had been promoted to management kept their positions when peace came, although men returning from the forces were usually offered back their old jobs. There were changes all round, however: former employees sometimes requested transfers to other departments which they felt would provide them with more interest or opportunity, and they expected shorter working hours. Store managers, for their part, took the opportunity to draw up more precise contracts of employment, or set up training schemes to refresh the memories of returning staff and to get the best out of them in a competitive commercial world.

The war had shaken up the old hierarchy of sales assistants, through which young men and women could slowly and carefully work their way up to senior positions. There was now a growing interest in bringing in capable people and training them directly for management. Even

37 *A letter from a supplier revealing the shortages of goods experienced in the post-war period*

new salesmen could be given more formal instruction, and promised regular promotion if they were up to standard. In 1953 a department store offered its incoming staff a six-month course in which practical work would be combined with 'technical instruction', a salary of £338 a year, a pension scheme, and shopping discounts. It was emphasized that 'a fine morale and atmosphere on the job' would be found, but that only those with 'a genuine interest in people and an even temperament' should apply.

38 *A chemist at work in his shop in the 1950s. His stockroom still has a Victorian appearance to it.*

The post-war village shop

The attraction of running a shop of one's own remained as strong as ever in the post-war period.

The owner is or appears to be his own master. His social position is affected and in his view enhanced by not belonging to the wage earning class. (Hermann Levy, *The Shops of Britain*, 1948)

Besides the pleasure of considering oneself to be a cut above the average shop assistant, as suggested here, the keeper of a village shop had the satisfaction of being regarded as a local oracle in many cases too:

The village chemist . . . is expected to have an encyclopaedic knowledge of every subject from cricket to theology.

At the post office:

The electricity supply people ring up. 'Do you know, please, whose supply is out of order and what is wrong with it?' The postmaster replies sarcastically that of course he knows everything . . . . This is one of the charms of the job. We do know everything. Although I took on the job during the war only in order to save the office from being closed, I cannot make up my mind to drop it now. **We sub-postmasters get first-hand information on all subjects, and the village conscience is in our keeping.** (Quotations written 1953 and 1950 from *The Countryman Book of Village Trades and Crafts*)

In small villages, the post-war phase was the last period when most items could still be bought locally, before increased use of cars and the growth of supermarkets changed the pattern of shopping. Between them, village shopkeepers and tradesmen calling from larger stores could supply the needs of people living in the district. A survey in 1947 of Luccombe, a small Somerset village with a population of about 200, revealed:

Regular deliveries of bread, meat, groceries, fish, and coal are made in the village; three wireless tradesmen call weekly, and two laundries once a fortnight, and . . . a representative of a big Minehead shoe retailer calls weekly with a van containing a choice of shoes . . . . For incidentals, there is the village shop, a very small grocery and general store with a cigarette and tobacco licence which depends for its custom entirely on the village. (W.J. Turner, *Exmoor Village*)

5 The 1950s and 1960s: Shopping for Convenience

Shops must make a profit to stay in business, but over the course of this century shop-owners have tried out different ways of persuading the customer to buy the goods on sale. Earlier, as we have seen, the emphasis was usually on high-quality, personal service, or on pressurized sales techniques. In the 20 years or so following the war, with many women going out to work, families owning cars, and a general speeding up of the pace of life, it became desirable to make shopping quick and easy for the customer. Shoppers no longer had the time to queue separately at each counter of a grocery store, or to wait for an asssistant to come and measure them for a dress. Shop managers began to turn their attention to eye-catching displays, self-selection of goods, and quick methods of payment. It was no longer economical, in many cases, to deliver goods to the customer, to accept payment on credit or to employ so many assistants.

The old dividing lines between shops serving rich and poor customers were breaking down, too, for rates of pay for manual and office workers had increased, allowing them to buy luxury goods, whereas the upper classes could, in general, no longer afford a host of servants and an extravagant living style. Buying goods on the 'never never' – hire purchase, where payments are spread out over several months or years – was a feature offered by many stores in the post-war period. This meant that families with lower incomes were more ready to commit themselves to buying expensive goods such as furniture or cookers, since they did not have to have all the money saved up beforehand, but could pay it in instalments.

'New Look' department stores

The need to rebuild bombed-out shops after the war gave their owners plenty of scope for designing stores on new lines. Hammond's of Hull, had a grand opening ceremony for their new department store in 1952 presided over by guest celebrity Dick Bentley, a well-known comedian. Fashion shows, competitions and special displays got the store off to a well-publicized start. One of its impressive new features was:

39 Hammond's new store of the 1950s, built to replace the building bombed in the war

a public address system, enabling announcements to be made, music broadcast and staff located. (*Daily Mail*, 1952)

Britain still looked to the United States for up-to-date ideas, and some shops sent representatives over to America to pick up design tips. They were impressed by the fact that major stores ran bargain and sale offers all year round to tempt shoppers, and that window displays were carefully planned and colour co-ordinated.

40 A window-dresser at work. Her work had now been recognized as a skilled job in its own right. Women window-dressers were encouraged to wear trousers to save them from embarrassment when clambering up step ladders in public view.

Window-dressing soon grew to be a job in its own right, and young people, including graduates from art college, were trained especially for display work. In the early post-war era, Liberty's of Regent Street decided to up-date their image by ripping out all the old-fashioned walnut panelling from their windows and employing an adventurous designer, Eric Lucking, to take charge of their displays. Materials were still in short supply, and the dummies on sale often stiff and dull to look at, so he made his own from wire, straw, waste timber, and any other materials he could obtain, using masks for faces. His designs were considered very daring at the time as he put both male and female models in the windows next to each other!

New product lines

When the restrictions on manufacturing and supplies were lifted in the mid-1950s product designs flourished. Robin Hartley of Heal's remembers that it was like 'coming up to the crest

41 Growing sales of televisions demanded new knowledge on the part of the assistants in electrical shops.

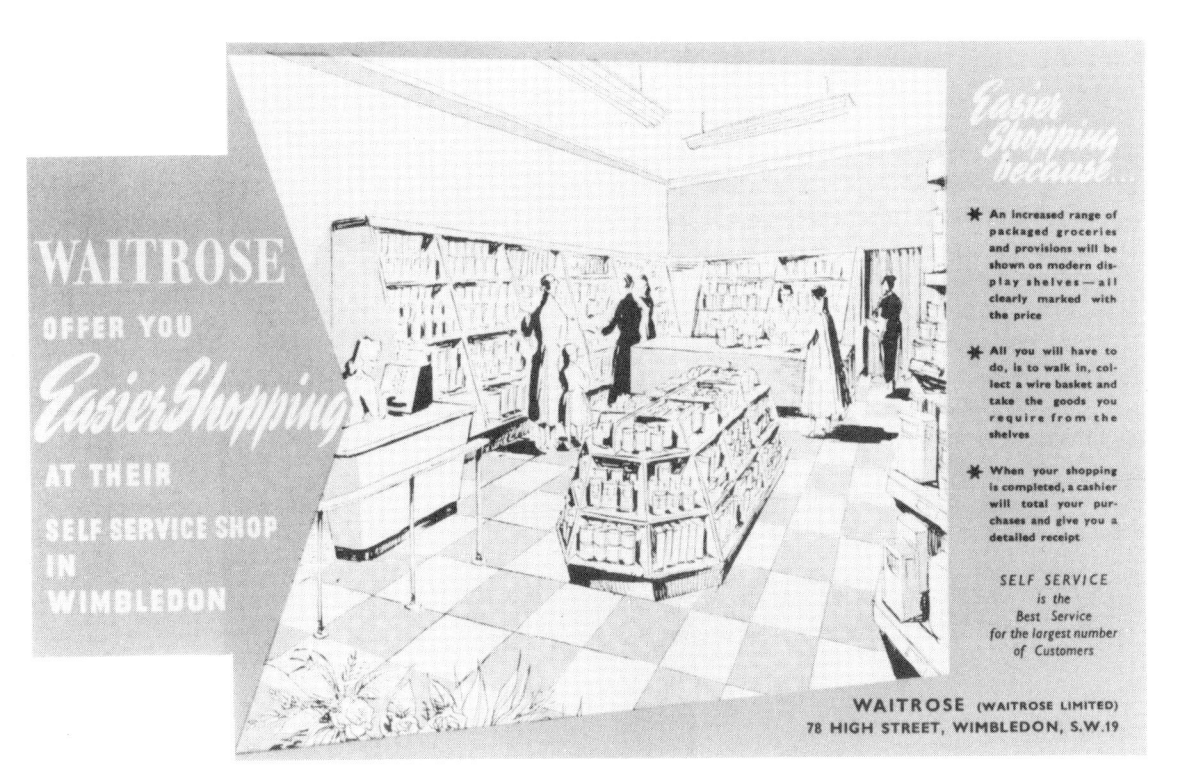

of the wave'. Furniture, glass-ware, and china all took on a new lease of life. The now wide use of synthetic materials such as plastic, nylon and polythene meant that there was an ever-increasing range of cheap household products. Shop assistants had to keep up to date in their knowledge of products. This was particularly true with electrical goods which, for the first time, became freely available at prices the general public could afford. Televisions, transistor radios, fridges, vacuum cleaners and, later, freezers and automatic washing machines became part of general household equipment.

The supermarket

But by far the biggest innovation to come into Britain from America was the supermarket. In the 1950s these began to spring up in towns and villages, till by 1961 there were over 700 in existence, with numbers increasing every day. They radically changed the work of the grocer. Previously, assistants had served behind counters, and, besides handing over packets and tins of food, their work had involved weighing butter, slicing bacon, cutting cheese, and

42 *A leaflet designed to help shoppers at Waitrose's new self-service supermarket in 1953 in Wimbledon*

packaging up many kinds of food which arrived 'loose', such as tea and biscuits. Some branded butters, biscuits, etc., had been sold ready packed for quite a time, but, in general, the grocer's job was to serve the customer personally with the quality and amount of food that he or she requested.

The supermarket layout meant that all the food was displayed and ready for the customer to pick up, put in a wire basket, and take to the check-out. Shoppers quickly learnt by familiarity with their favourite supermarket where to find products, and the management was equally quick in learning to tempt shoppers – and often their children – to buy extra items such as sweets, crisps, and magazines in prominent positions or at the check-out itself. The assistant's job became more commonly that of a shelf-filler or a check-out operator, responsible for adding up the cost of the goods chosen. It became possible for unskilled assistants to find work more easily, since the training required was not so great.

Supermarkets were built on a larger and larger scale; many customers now drove to a shopping centre, and collected all their groceries, meat, greengroceries and bread in one trip. This made it more difficult for the small local provisions stores to survive, since they could not offer such a wide variety, and, not being able to order stock in such large quanties as the supermarkets, could not buy in their goods so cheaply.

In the early days of supermarkets, managers were often very dubious as to whether or not they would be popular with the public. When Waitrose opened its first self-service supermarket at Streatham in 1955, it offered a free shopping list pad to its customers; supplies quickly ran out, so it gave away tins of peaches instead, and the takings for the first week were double those estimated. Nor was there any difficulty in finding staff, as had been feared.

A huge poster was put in the window . . . saying

43 *The hat and coat department in Cavendish's stores, Cheltenham; the surroundings are still spacious, as in the early days of department stores, but now assistants are less in evidence and customers are encouraged to browse for themselves.*

that recruiting would take place at 10am. . . . Mr Tobias [the manager] went alone to do the interviewing and when he arrived found two hundred people queueing outside. Working in a self-service shop was a novelty that had a great attraction. There were no tables available, so Mr Tobias fixed up trestles on step-ladders for the applicants to fill in application forms. (*John Lewis Gazette*, August 1974)

Fashion boutiques and clothes departments

The selling of clothes changed, too, in the 1960s. Young people with money to spend were looking to buy colourful and inexpensive clothes; the 'Swinging Sixties' was an era for fast-changing fashions and crazy designs, such as mini-skirts, paper dresses, and boots with holes in them. Fashion-conscious teenagers wanted to buy an outfit today wear it to a party tonight, and then forget about it tomorrow. The old system of a well-trained and exceedingly polite assistant showing each customer the clothes available, advising her on style and fit, and sending the garment to be altered if necessary was now thought tedious and fussy by the younger generation. Many young people with some available finance opened their own 'boutiques', small clothes shops which sold individual designs and fashions at reasonable prices. 'Pop' music was played, and these shops became a social meeting place; in London the King's Road area and Carnaby Street became famous at this time for their clothes shops, and for the 'beautiful people', including film and pop stars, who visited them.

Even in the more sedate and cautious stores, workrooms were closing down, with loss of jobs for those staff employed to make clothes to order or to carry out alterations. It became acceptable for the customer to look through racks of clothes without much in the way of assistance, which meant that departmental managers had to ensure that the displays were clearly set out and sized.

It was at this time that the pattern of buying almost all clothes ready made finally became fixed. Before the First World War, nearly all garments had been made-to-measure, with the exception of some coats and cheaper blouses and underwear. Afterwards, women had begun to choose more of their clothes from the ready-to-wear selection which were being manufactured in larger quantities. With these, the latest fashions could be bought and worn straight away – no lengthy waits and tedious hours of being measured and pinned up. Men, more conservative in their tastes, and expecting their clothes to last longer, had still gone to their tailors for a new suit, but, even as early as the 1930s, 'off-the peg' suits could be bought. Gradually it became more common for men to shop in this way until, from the 1960s onwards, it became a symbol of luxury to order a made-to-measure shirt, suit or jacket.

Shop-lifting and security systems

Having goods laid out for shoppers to pick up meant, of course, shop-lifting problems increased. In the 1950s and 1960s security systems were set up in major stores. These sometimes consisted of secret alarm bells or coloured lights which the assistants could press to bring the Security Officer to help them if they thought a customer was stealing. In *Heal's Employees' Guide* of 1962, it was made very clear that only a senior member of staff could challenge a customer, that this should be done (for legal reasons) outside the shop, and with the minimum of fuss so as not to cause a noticeable disturbance:

The challenge should be made discreetly and politely in the form of a request to return to the shop. 'I have reason to believe that you have goods for which no payment has been made. Would you please return with me to the shop?'

Quick and self-service shopping also brought the need for efficient ways of paying for goods. However, although some efforts were made to rationalize the procedure in the 1950s and 1960s, methods were varied and often complex until electric and electronic tills became widely available in the 1970s and 1980s. The 'Lamson tube', an old favourite, was still in use in many large shops and department stores. This consisted of a series of tubes connecting each part of the shop to the cash office. A bill was written out by the assistant, placed in a metal cylinder with the customer's money, and put into the tube where it was whisked back to the cashier by suction. In due course the cylinder would come rattling down again with the bill stamped and any change enclosed. In other places the assistant had to take the bill and money to another assistant at a cash desk nearby, as is still the practice in a number of shoe shops today. Cash registers, where used, were worked manually, and a ticket would flash up in the display window at the top to show the amount the assistant had rung up.

Conditions of work

Working conditions for shop assistants were changing at this time. The Offices, Shops and Railway Premises Act of 1963 set legal standards for the safety and hygiene of shops. This gave assistants basic safeguards, such as a comfortable temperature in which to work (not less than 60.8 degrees Fahrenheit), adequate ventilation, lighting, and cleaning of the premises. Toilet, washing, and drinking water facilities had to be provided, and also places where staff could hang up their clothes. Most stores had been offering good facilities to their employees for some time in this respect, but the Act gave legal support to this and obliged all shops (apart from those personally or family-run) to keep up to standard.

The hours worked by assistants had been reduced considerably since the early part of the century, so that in the 1960s the average week consisted of about 40 to 45 hours. Paid holidays were not as generous in length as they are today, often only one or two weeks per year, but this was also the norm in other areas, such as office and factory work. But pay was, in general, far lower than that for the manufacturing or building trades, for instance. Given that working in a shop had lost some of its middle-class status, and that manual workers could earn better wages, a career in retailing as a counter assistant no longer seemed such an appealing prospect. In the mid-1960s, a junior shop assistant could earn as little as £6 a week, while a teenage factory worker might be on a wage of £20. Girls could be particularly apathetic about their work; Joan Blackshaw, now managing a shoe shop, remembers:

When I left school either you went into a factory or a shop, if you didn't have higher education. You thought of it as a stopgap to tide you over till you got married.

Relaxed attitudes towards staff and customers

By the 1960s working in a shop had come to be regarded more as a temporary or casual job, rather than as a career for life. In many stores there was less skill involved in selling, and sometimes less chance of promotion, since leading stores and multiples were now bringing in graduates to train them for management. The

---

44 *Cover of the staff magazine at Heal's, designed to keep employees up to date with company news*

UNSOLICITED TRIBUTE in a recent Guardian

Heal's please copy. Our Warsaw scout reports that State bed-sitterdom has grown so constricted that a new device is on the market. It's called the 'chandelier bed'. When you get up in the morning you haul a rope and the bed rises to the ceiling with a light bulb attached to one leg.

'reign of terror' imposed by the old family bosses was over in many cases. This meant more informality and freedom for the staff, but also a loss of team spirit and loyalty to the firm. Robin Hartley remembers the changes that took place at Heal's furniture shop when Sir Ambrose Heal died in 1959. Mr Hartley himself had joined the firm in 1956 for a wage of £4 12s. 6d., first as a craftsman then as a salesman. Ambrose Heal was a dominating presence:

He used to potter round the shop with his walking stick, and occasionally he would whack something down and say, 'Get that out of my shop!'

The attitude of the staff towards him:

... wasn't really fear. It was utter respect. You didn't do anything if you thought he wouldn't like it.

But after he died:

Suddenly, I didn't have to wear a black jacket and pin-striped trousers. We were allowed to wear lounge suites of a dark colour. We no longer had to come in through the front door and be inspected by Mr Chapman, the Apprentice Master, who could, if we were looking scruffy, send us home and not pay us till we came back looking not scruffy.

Department stores, who were losing many younger customers to the boutiques and chain stores, often tried to keep their own style of quality and personal service to attract a different type of customer. Staff were still encouraged to think of the customers respectfully, as *Colson's Staff Guide* of the 1950s reminds assistants:

A customer is not an interruption of our work – she is the purpose of it. . . . A customer is not someone to argue or match wits with. Nobody ever wins an argument with a customer.

However, such reminders would have been unnecessary in an earlier age, when it could cost an assistant his or her job to ignore a customer or to argue with her! Another guideline, in Brown and Muff's Rules for 1964, tries to find a way of convincing staff that they can be polite without losing their dignity or being servile:

Receive all customers in the store as you would welcome a guest in your own home.

If you compare these pieces of advice with others from earlier dates quoted in the book (see pages 20, 21 and 33), you will see clearly the changing attitude between staff and customers.

Social facilities

In the 1950s and 1960s, though, social facilities for staff were still lively and well-supported. Heal's boasted a social club with a bar, table-tennis, games and dances, plus 'record playing sessions', all for one shilling per annum. Dingle's, of Exeter, organized outings and kept a beach hut at the resort of Dawlish Warren for their staff. Harrod's could provide entertainment for every sort of taste, with a choral society, bingo, cabaret, children's parties, sports days, and a staff magazine. But the pattern was changing. From the late 1960s onwards, shop staff began to keep their work and social lives separate. Loyalty to the firm was diminishing partly because jobs were easy to come by, and expectations of wages and working conditions higher.

45 *A party given for the children of staff at Brown & Muff's, Bradford, 1958*

6 The 1970s and On: the Electronic Age

Today, shopping remains an essential part of daily life, catering both for people's basic needs and their desires for luxury and fashionable goods. Although the economic recession in the 1970s has made commercial activities in Britain difficult generally, yet our expectations are still as they have been since the war - that we shall buy more consumer goods, the latest fashions in clothes and the most up-to-date electrical and electronic products. In fact, despite the problems of unemployment, we bought 8 per cent more goods from retail outlets in 1982 than we did in 1978. Shops, therefore, are constantly trying to improve their sales by new layouts, more sophisticated equipment and eye-catching promotions. Sales, which have been a popular feature of shopping throughout the century, have become more numerous and frequent. It is now common practice for shops to have summer as well as winter sales, and sometimes even 'mid-season' sales, too. Cheaper goods are often bought in to attract customers with low prices, although by law they can only be sold as 'special purchase' rather than sales goods. In the 1980s, too, there has been a swing away from the more casual attitudes of the 1960s and 1970s, back to the old idea of helpful personal service in shops.

Decimalization

One of the first major changes in the 1970s was decimalization. On 15 February 1971 the nation switched from using pounds, shillings and pence for currency (12 pence to one shilling, and 20 shillings to one pound) to the simpler 100 pence to the pound that we have today. In shops, staff had to be trained for weeks in advance to adapt to new procedures. In the larger stores, booklets and question sheets were issued so that the assistants could be drilled, with exercises like these:

What do you write between the £ sign and the decimal point? *Must* you always have a figure between the £ sign and the decimal point?
How do you write the new halfpenny in figures?
Please subtract £19.98½ from £45

Cash registers, too, had to be altered to display the new pounds and pence. Once the change-over had taken place, most people found it much easier to work with the new decimal figures.

The introduction of computers

The new electronic and computerized equipment that has been introduced into shops in recent years is also aimed at making the staff's work more streamlined and efficient. Computers were used for stock control in some stores in the 1960s, but they were very expensive to instal and run, and extremely bulky, needing a special room to house them. Today, computer systems are playing an increasing part in pricing, ordering, and payment. Many supermarket tills are now linked to a computer, some of them with

---

46 *A check-out assistant (lady, seated) operating the new laser scanning check-out system, aided by computer, at Elston's Cash and Carry store, Minehead*

laser beams incorporated to scan bar codes on products, which the computer will translate into a price and transmit back to the check-out. Obviously, staff have to be trained to work computerized tills, but the procedures are not difficult, and may help to cut down on errors that assistants make when entering up the prices. (A consumer survey carried out in the early 1980s found that a large percentage of supermarket bills had mistakes on them.)

A computer is only as good as the programme devised for it, however, and there are still plenty of hiccups where ordering and supplies for shops are concerned. Mr Robin Hartley, of Heal's furniture shop, comments:

In 1971 we had a cumbersome computer system which couldn't understand our bedding factory. We now have a more powerful system – but guess what it still can't understand? Yes, the bedding factory!

Combatting shoplifting

It has become increasingly difficult, despite closed-circuit television and other electronic security devices, for shops to keep down the levels of shop-lifting. In 1981 it was estimated that the loss represented about 2 per cent in terms of prices of goods, and that shop-lifting was increasing by about 20 per cent every year. The cost of supplying security systems ran at £1½ million nationwide in that year. Highly trained store detectives are now widely used. A group of chain stores might have 'mobile security officers' who will cover several shops in a locality on their rounds, whereas the larger chain stores and department stores will have a regular team of men and women at work. In 1977, the writer Polly Toynbee accompanied for two days a detective on duty at Marks and Spencer's, Oxford Street and published an account of her visit. The detective was one of a squad of 13, some of whom had previously been in the police force, while others had been recruited from regular sales staff. They were able to contact each other and the assistants by 'bleepers' should suspicious – or even dangerous – circumstances arise.

We watch their eyes. You can see if they're interested in the goods, or if they're looking round them. Most of all we watch their hands. Something can be gone in a minute . . . . Sometimes I hear the sound of bags rattling oddly, and I prick up my ears.

Pam Phillips, the detective, made several arrests, including a man with 'a mean-looking face', who had to be chased up and down stairs, two Egyptian women, who openly filled up their bags with groceries, and an old Persian man, whom the manager decided to release on grounds of age:

We don't want any heart attacks. I'd hate to have to resuscitate. (*The Way We Live Now*)

Most shop-lifters *are* prosecuted, however, since the stores find the problem such a major one that it is impossible to make allowances except in very rare circumstances. 'If people are caught, then they must pay the penalty', says Mr Quinlan, the manager of a Woolworth's store. Some of the stealing that goes on is, and always has been, carried out by the assistants themselves. It is common for staff to be asked to leave their shopping bags with the porter at the staff entrance, and to check out carefully goods and receipts for their own purchases when they leave.

In small shops it can be far more difficult for the shopkeeper to detect theft and take action against the culprit. When there is only one assistant on duty, it is not easy to follow a customer suspected of theft out of the shop. (No conviction can normally be made unless it can be proved that the person left the shop without intending to pay for goods.) If violence is threatened, the lone shopkeeper is not usually in a position to deal with the situation easily. Most shops run or attended by one person try to rely on prevention, by having all the goods where they can be seen easily and by taking care not to be distracted by, for instance, a request to fetch an item out of the window.

The small retailer

Running a shop of one's own is still a very popular occupation. Many of the clothes boutiques set up in the 1960s did not survive the fierce competition, but businesses selling antiques, delicatessen foods, health foods, books and crafts have expanded greatly in numbers. Some of these are run on a part-time basis, suiting the hours of work that can be put in by women with dependent families, people with other occupations or craft-workers. Gwen Baker is a professional singer, but she also keeps a music shop which is open part-time:

The shop itself may not be very profitable, but I meet some really interesting people here, and I can order my own music at trade price.

In such shops, satisfaction is often found as much in buying in the goods as in selling them; antiques must be tracked down, catalogues must be scanned for interesting books and local craft fairs visited. Unfortunately the owners of these businesses are often too hopeful and idealistic in their approach to retailing and inexperienced in

47 *Running a shop part-time is a popular occupation, which is the way Mrs Baker's music agency in St Peter Port, Guernsey, is organized.*

estimating costs and custom. Hermann Levy's comment in *The Shops of Britain* (1948) remains as true today as ever:

Many shops which should go out of business remain alive by changing hands.

Nevertheless, it is a perennial inspiration to many people to plan for the time when they, too, can open a shop of their choice.

48 *This cartoon takes a wry look at the changing fortunes of small shops from the 1960s until the present day. Provisions shops run by immigrants from India, Pakistan, Italy, the West Indies and Poland are now a common feature of shopping in Britain, especially in urban areas. Often all the members of the family work in the shop and the hours of opening are long. Shops such as these can supply specialist ingredients and goods for other immigrants of the same nationality.*

The changing staff/customer relationship

In the larger stores, training schemes, conditions of employment and attitudes to work vary widely.

Mrs Pepper, Personnel Manager of Sainsbury's, Exeter explains:

Because we open late on certain evenings, we need staff to work what are called 'unsociable hours' . . .

She often has to interview as many as 30 people for four or five jobs.

Mature women are often more conscientious and responsible in their work. I'm looking for staff who can move quickly, physically, too. You can tell by somebody's walk how they're going to react to the job – if they walk at a snail's pace, then they'll work the same way!

In general, there has been an increase of emphasis on politeness and good service over the last few years. This is partly because jobs have been in short supply, so that applicants need to be well-motivated and enthusiastic about retail work before they will be taken on. It is also partly because the general public are becoming more discriminating, as Joan Blackshaw, manager of Ridler's shoe shop, Minehead, comments:

At the end of the 1960s, service took a dive, with self-selection coming in, and large overheads

49 *Assistants working at food counters are trained to a high standard of hygiene nowadays. Note the protective caps, and the wash basin near to hand.*

cutting down the numbers of staff that a shop could employ. At first it was a novelty, but now the public are getting fed up with it and the attitude of, 'If you can't find it, don't ask me, Madam, because I don't know.'

The 'Customer Policy' produced by the firm, Mister Minit, which runs shoe-repairing and key-cutting services in large stores, reflects the attitude that many retailers are now trying to encourage:

Be friendly – show the customer you care.
Be alert to customer needs – look – show – speak.
Be eager – promote all services.
Be proud – present your work.
Think ahead – invite the customer back.

Recruitment and training

The high level of unemployment has meant a rush of hopeful candidates every time a job in a shop is offered. Woolworth's stores, who in the 1960s found it hard to recruit enough staff, now have a waiting list of people wanting full or part-time work, and make a policy of looking for good school or academic qualifications from those who apply. Mr Quinlan, Manager of Woolworth's Minehead, says:

Age is relatively unimportant, as we can train them on. We're looking for staff who are bright and cheerful, and who enjoy working with other people. And they must be prepared to put the needs of the customer first – *always.*

Although they offer less personal service in their stores from the angle of helping with selection since their 'cash-wrap operation' was introduced, with its check-out type pay desks, they encourage their staff to learn as much as possible about the products they sell, and to direct customers to another supplier for any goods that are not in stock. As Mr Quinlan says:

At first the public didn't like the cash-wrap system. But now it's a more streamlined and efficient operation. People don't have to queue to be served any more, and the staff don't have to have eyes in the back of their heads as they used to when there were island counters with customers on each side.

Joan Blackshaw also reports a growing enthusiasm among staff to learn more about their work and to take responsibility.

Recently three assistants volunteered to give up a Sunday to go to a shoe fair in London, with expenses covered, but no pay. It wouldn't have happened a few years ago.

Training schemes in all branches of retail trade are carefully planned, and staff from small shops can join in by, for instance, taking a special course offered by a manufacturer. Larger stores offer opportunities for school and college leavers to go directly into training for a particular position, such as selection, administration, or personnel. Marks and Spencer's, for example, offer suitable candidates a starting salary (at the time of writing) of £7,500 and an 18-month initial training scheme to become a departmental manager.

Pay

Pay for the majority of shop assistants is not usually so favourable, however. It can start at as little as £59 a week for a 16-year-old counter hand, and rise to only £120 or so for the higher grades of shop supervisors. However, job security can be very important today, and many people prefer to accept relatively low wages in return for a steady job with promotion prospects. In rural areas, especially, staff tend to stay longer in employment and develop a sense of teamwork and loyalty to the store. In the cities, problems of quick staff turnover still arise and wages may be a contributory factor here: with a high urban cost of living, many workers with families find that they

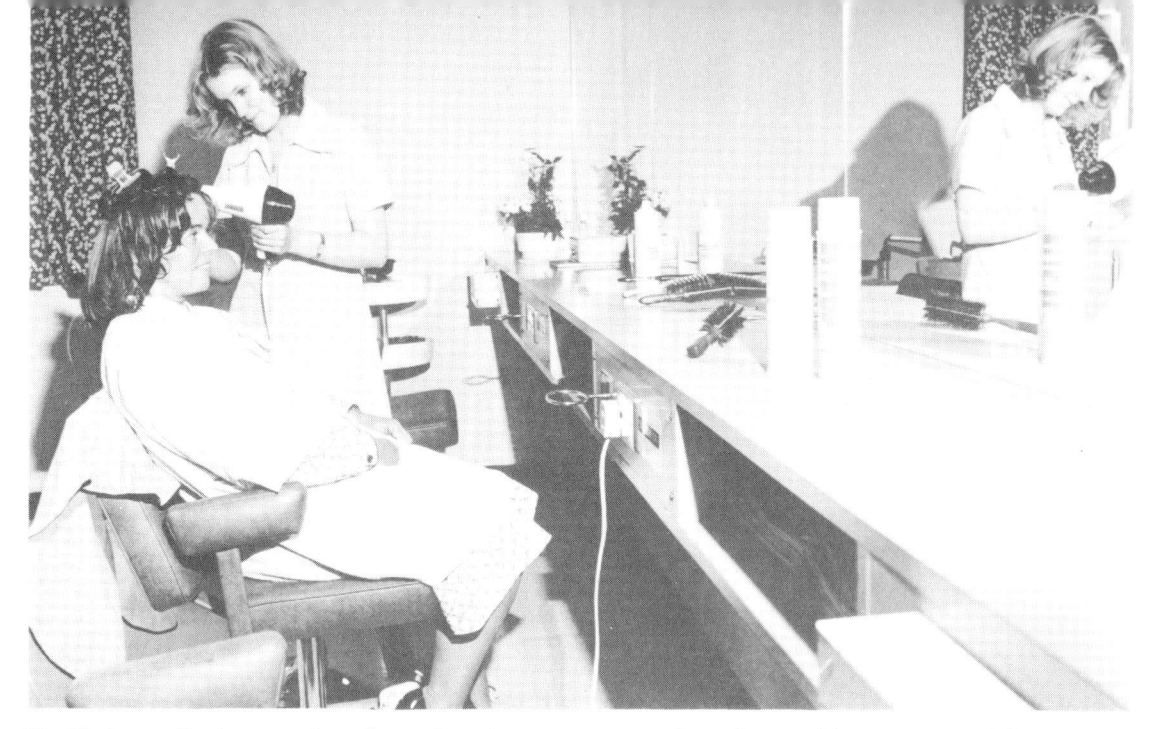

50 *Today, staff enjoy many benefits, such as the inexpensive hair-dressing service offered by Marks and Spencer's to their employees during the lunch break.*

cannot manage well on a shop assistant's pay. Therefore, stores often advertise for assistants aged 25 and under, who are more likely to be able to manage on the rates offered, and many of these move on before long. Robin Hartley of Heal's comments:

The turnover is enormous. I don't bother to learn people's names any more because they're gone so soon.

Looking to the future

It is hard to predict the changes that will take place in shop work in the future. However, it seems likely that this trend towards encouraging personal service will continue. It may well be that staff will be graded more precisely, and that some will perform routine and mechanical jobs, such as checking out goods at the till, whereas others will be thoroughly trained to know all about the products on sale and to advise the customer about purchases. While the giant superstores and hypermarkets will probably expand and provide very useful 'one-stop' shopping, undoubtedly the small shops will hold their own since they can provide a better service and sometimes more original goods for sale. Certain cities, such as Cambridge and Edinburgh, have encouraged smaller retailers to set up businesses in the town centres, so that the main shopping precincts are not merely showplaces for the large multiple stores. To have smaller, privately owned shops gives character to a town or city. Street markets, too, show no signs of dying out, and are ever popular with customers for buying fruit, vegetables and bargain goods such as material and china, second-hand and craft items.

It is also possible that in the future we shall have to re-define the meaning of the word 'shop' itself. Already more and more people are shopping with credit cards, which means that the whole transaction is completed without cash changing hands, and it is expected that soon, through computer and television link-ups, customers will be able to order and pay for what they want without having to set a foot outside their own front doors. Such operations are in very limited use at the moment, but it is likely that they will become more widespread. Shop assistants themselves may come to be known as 'customer advisors' when credit cards, computers and laser terminals take over the actual process of buying.

Glossary

A.R.P. Wardens (Air Raid Patrol Wardens), trained volunteers in local streets and places of work, who would make sure that all the rules, such as blacking-out lights at night, were obeyed, and would be on hand to help if bombs fell

bespoke refers to clothes or goods which are specially made or ordered for a customer

boutique small shop with an individual selection of goods

branded goods an example of branded goods would be that of tea sold in a packet with the importer's name on it, rather than being supplied loose to the grocer

cash-wrap method of selling where goods are taken by the customer to a check-out or cash-point and the assistant wraps them and takes the money at the same time

charabanc an early form of motor bus or coach, often with an open top

cicerone a superior type of shop assistant who acted as a guide to customers, greeting them at the door and taking them to the right department to be served by the assistants there

closed-circuit T.V. a system of keeping watch on the activities of customers through positioning cameras in the store; the pictures are screened on T.V. monitors placed where assistants within the store or security officers behind the scenes can see them.

distemper a kind of cheap paint, used particularly on walls

embargo a prohibition upon trading or shipping of goods

emporium used here to mean a large store; the Oxford dictionary gives one definition as 'A pompous name for a shop'!

fire-watching looking out for fires that might have been started by bombs falling and exploding

gig a light, horse-drawn carriage, with two wheels only

landau a horse-drawn carriage, four-wheeled, and with a top that could be opened up

living-in until the First World War, shop assistants were often compelled to live on the shop premises or in nearby lodging houses. They were then available for long hours of work, and their behaviour could be checked continually by their employers.

overheads costs of running a shop or store

pre-fabs small, one-storey houses that could be put up quickly, usually with asbestos roofs, to replace bomb-damaged homes

rationing in both World Wars, the Government took control of supplies of certain types of food, and allowed each person to buy no more than fixed amounts of these. This was to try and overcome the problems that arose with shortages, since overseas trading was severely restricted and some materials, such as wool and metal, were needed to make supplies for the armed forces.

tea-dances a popular form of entertainment in the 1920s and 1930s, in which participants arrived during the afternoon to enjoy both tea and dancing in a ballroom or restaurant. A live orchestra was usually provided.

Utility clothing to prevent extravagance and conserve supplies of materials, the Government introduced controls over the prices, materials and styles of clothes during the Second World War. Clothes manufactured while this scheme was enforced were known as 'Utility' garments.

Date List

1860s	First department stores open in France	1950s	First supermarkets open in Britain
1891	Marks and Spencer Penny Bazaar starts in Wigan	1963	Offices, Shops and Railways Premises Act introduced, laying down minimum conditions for staff facilities and working environment
	National Union of Shop Assistants formed		
1898	*Daily Chronicle* arouses public interest in plight of shop-workers by publicizing its investigation into shop conditions	1970	Equal Pay Act enforced to ensure that women should be paid the same wage as men for the same job
		1971	Decimal currency introduced
1913	Strikes by shop-workers, especially in South Wales, for better pay	1974	Health and Safety at Work Act, giving further measures for the protection of employees in terms of dangerous machinery etc. in shops and other places of work
1914-18	First World War. Many shop-workers leave to join armed forces; trade decreases with staff and goods shortages.		
1918	Food-rationing introduced	1975	Sex Discrimination Act. This, coupled with the Race Discrimination Act of 1968 makes it illegal to discriminate against any employee or would-be employee on grounds of their sex or race.
1939-45	Second World War. Shops have to cope with less staff and German bombing raids. Rationing of many products by Government, making work more complex in shops due to ration books and coupons.		
1945	Minimum scale of wages enforced	1970s and 1980s	Widespread introduction of computerized and electronic equipment into shops
1952	End of food rationing		

Books for Further Reading

General books on shops and shop-workers

Alison Adburgham, *Shops and Shopping*, Allen and Unwin, 1981
Dorothy Davis, *A History of Shopping*, RKP, 1961
Lee Holcombe, *Victorian Ladies at Work*, David & Charles, 1973
Renée Huggett, *History in Focus: Shops*, B.T. Batsford, 1969

Sources of extracts

P.C. Hoffman, *They Also Serve*, Porcupine Press, 1949
Margaret Penn, *Manchester Fourteen Miles*, Futura reprint, 1982
Elizabeth Seegar (ed.), *The Countryman Book of Village Trades and Crafts*, David and Charles, 1978
Gilbert Stone, *Women War Workers*, 1917

Books about specific shops

Alison Adburgham, *Liberty's*, George Allen & Unwin, 1975
Rowan Bentall, *My Store of Memories*, W.H. Allen, 1974 (Bentall's, Kingston-upon-Thames)
D.W. Peel, *A Garden in the Sky*, W.H. Allen, 1960 (Barker's of Kensington)
G. Rees, *St Michael – A History of Marks and Spencer*, Weidenfeld & Nicolson, 1969
H.D. Wilcock (ed.), *Brown & Chester*, 1947

Index

air-raids 19, 34, 39-41
American influences 21-2, 47-50
apprentices 8, 10-11

'bosses' and managers 13, 21, 38, 43, 52-3

'carriage trade' 6
cash registers 28, 52, 54
'cash-wrap' 59
cheating customers 23
check-out assistant 49, 55, 60
commission 15
computers 54-5, 60
coupons 43
credit 17, 42, 47
   cards 60
customer relations 10, 12, 20, 33, 41-2, 45, 51, 53, 58-9

decimalization 54
deliveries 32, 37, 45, 47
dismissal 12-13
dress 14
dressmakers 10-11

early-closing campaign 15
electronic tills 51, 54-5
emporium 6, 19
escalators 28

fines 15, 16
fires 16, 40

gas lighting 14

health problems 17

hire purchase 47
holiday pay 15, 32

immigrant shopkeepers 19, 57

'Lamson' tube 51-2
'living-in' 15-17

management 7, 33, 38-9, 43-4, 52
manager, see bosses and managers
markets 5, 12, 60

pay 7, 15, 27, 44, 52, 59-60
pedlars 5
production of goods 8, 27, 42, 43, 48-9

rationing 19, 35, 41-3
rules of conduct 12, 20, 23, 32-3, 52

sales 19, 47, 34
salesmanship 26
shop-lifting 51, 55-6
shops
   antique 56
   books 56
   butcher 18, 19, 31
   chemist 44, 45
   clothing 10, 11, 33, 51; see also dressmakers
   confectioners 8-9, 19, 25, 27
   crafts 56
   dairy 9, 27
   delicatessen 56
   department stores 7, 8, 11, 12, 20, 53
   drapery 11
   fishmongers 31

furnishing 43
greengrocers 19
grocery 14, 18, 19, 23, 33, 43, 45, 47, 49
health food 56
hypermarket 60
lingerie 25
multiple stores 7, 12, 16, 18, 27, 60
parlour 6, 8, 17, 18
pawnbrokers 28
perfume 9
post office 45
shoe 9, 29, 45
sweet, see confectioners
tea-rooms 25
village 7, 17, 18, 45
social facilities 33, 53
   clubs 21, 30-1
   drama 31
   outings 13, 31, 53
   sports 21
store detectives 55

trade unions 20-1
training of staff 26-7, 32, 33, 43-4, 53, 55, 59
transport 7, 17, 32, 37, 43, 47, 50

uniforms, see dress

war work 18-19, 35-9
welfare of staff 29, 52
window display 28, 47
women in shops 7, 17, 18-19, 36-8, 43
work
   hours 7, 14, 15, 52, 58
   seasonal and temporary 8, 12-13, 52